TRAGEDY OF KINGS

The Enemies of Martin Luther King, Jr. and the Economics of Hate

Dan Taber

"As a crime fiction writer, I know you can't make this stuff up. As an American, I'm troubled that it is still so entirely believable—and topical—some fifty years later."
—Edgar Award Winner Theresa Schwegel, on *Tragedy of Kings*

Sign up for my mailing list at http://dantaber.com/free/ and receive a free excerpt of my upcoming sci-fi adventure

www.dantaber.com

Library of Congress Cataloging-in-Publication Data
Names: Taber, Dan - author.
Title: A Tragedy of Kings: The Enemies of Martin Luther King Jr.
and the Economics of Hate

ISBN: 9781723711831

Edited by Brenda Croghan
Cover design by Dennis Choinski

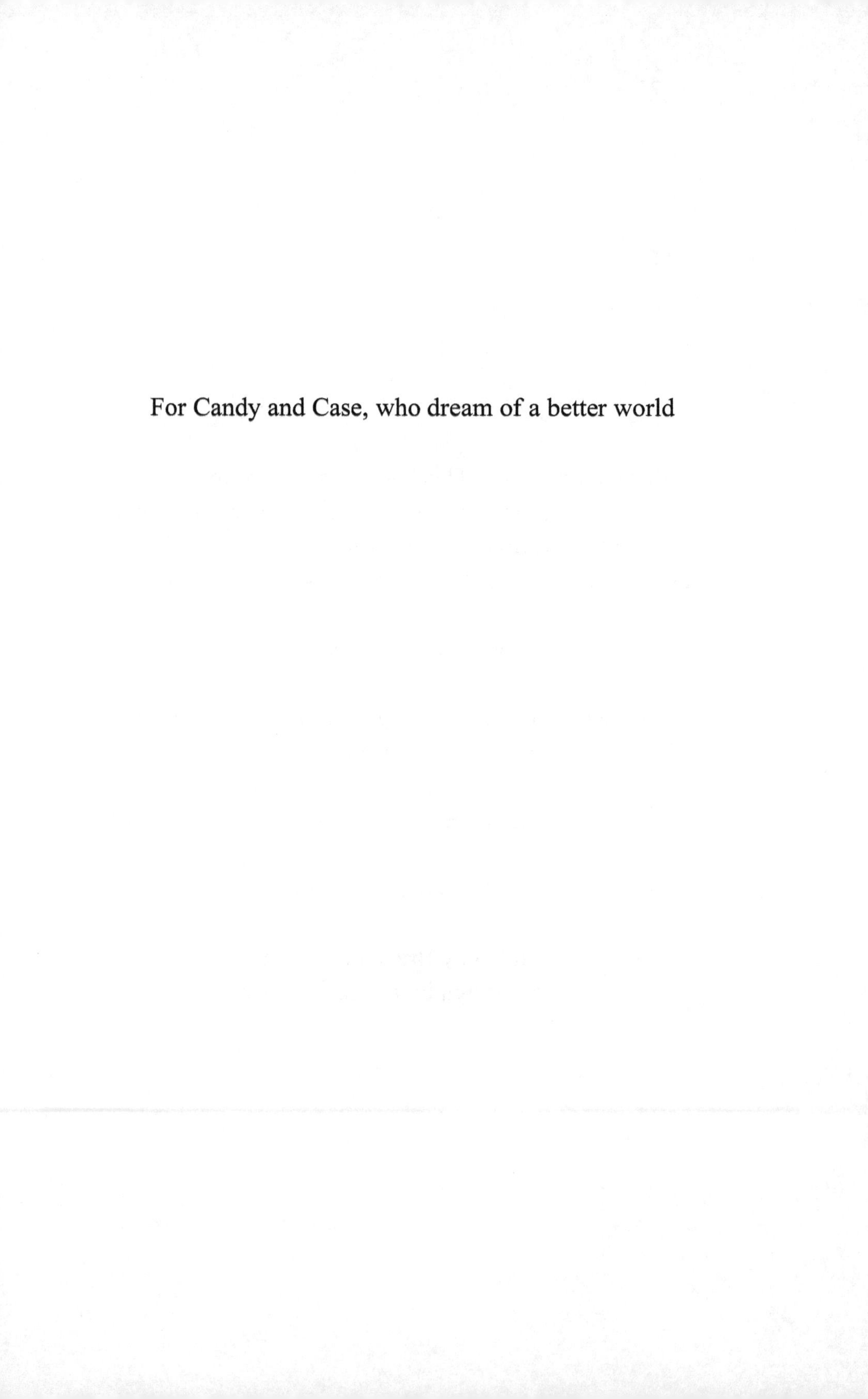

For Candy and Case, who dream of a better world

Contents

Introduction

It took thirty years for a jury to confirm what the family of the greatest American human rights leader had already concluded: government agencies were guilty of conspiring to assassinate Martin Luther King, Jr. The existence of *King v. Jowers and Other Unknown Co-Conspirators* is not fake news. The largely unpublicized civil trial occurred in 1999. During three-and-a-half weeks of proceedings, nearly seventy witnesses contributed to implicate the FBI, Army Intelligence and Memphis Police, among others. Despite an abundance of evidence in support of the verdict, the Department of Justice and its advocates attempted to reject the trial's validity.

Any inquiring reader can make an independent decision regarding the truth of King's assassination by examining three events that led to an array of determinations. Combined, *King v. Jowers* . . ., Senator Church's Committee on Intelligence Overreach, and the House Select Committee on Assassinations (HSCA) provide objective insight.

As new evidence has surfaced, writers have increasingly challenged the traditional view established by the HSCA that James Earl Ray operated as King's lone assassin. When one delves deep into this issue it becomes clear that many people were involved. Americans are well aware that southern authorities and white supremacists opposed King's campaign. Many are also conscious of J. Edgar Hoover's contempt for the peaceful dreamer, which several politicians and business owners echoed. Less recognized, Lyndon Johnson's apparent goodwill toward Dr. King dissipated when the two differed regarding Vietnam and the president's financial interests. Intensive examination of all participants exposes who was truly responsible for the assassination. But that is only half the story. The other half reveals a link between civil rights opponents and economic suppression, a link that has trickled down through the years to impact every American today.

Chapter 1
A Spark of Change

The year 1955 brought momentous beginnings. From New York to California, Chuck Berry and Little Richard electrified young revelers with an exciting new style called rock and roll. The United States military established a foothold in South Vietnam. Mary Maxwell Gates gave birth to a boy who would help usher in the information age. As these seeds stirred the future of America, Rosa Parks sparked a movement when she refused to give up her bus seat to a white man in Birmingham, Alabama.[1] Her courage inspired Martin Luther King's campaign to address racial and economic inequality.

Eight years later, King had become a well known figure in the United States, to many a hero, although others resented his humanitarian efforts.

In 1963, the Governor of Alabama, George Wallace crowed, "In the name of the greatest people that have ever trod this Earth, I draw the line in the dust and toss the gauntlet before the feet of tyranny, and I say segregation now, segregation tomorrow, segregation

---

[1] Additional women arrested the same year for violating local bus segregation laws include Claudette Colvin, Aurelia Browder, and Mary Louise Smith.

forever." His ironic reference to an invisible tyranny did not stifle his later presidential bid.

Soon thereafter, "Bull" Connor, the Commissioner of Public Safety in Birmingham, Alabama, authorized the use of fire hoses and attack dogs on peaceful protestors and children during a march King had organized to promote justice.

Congressmen including Strom Thurmond and Robert Byrd expressed repeated prejudiced resistance to equal rights. Yet Dr. King's most persistent adversary was the Director of the FBI, J. Edgar Hoover. Not long before King was awarded the 1964 Nobel Peace Prize, Hoover discourteously denounced him as "the most notorious liar in the country." In a conversation with Lyndon Johnson, Hoover expressed the fear that King was "an instrument in the hands of subversive forces seeking to undermine our nation." A letter from the FBI revealed the agency's desire to "neutralize him." FBI agent William Sullivan said that Hoover hated King and Robert Kennedy more than anyone else.

Dr. King's open disapproval of the occasions on which law enforcement committed malicious acts against black citizens or failed to address racially motivated crimes provoked the animosity of powerful authorities, like Hoover, who ironically engaged in unlawful activity for a significant portion of his tenure, without ever being convicted.[2] Likewise, King made few friends at the white house when he objected to the policies adopted by the presidential administration of Lyndon Johnson. On April 4, 1967, one year to the day before his assassination, King referred to the American government as "The greatest purveyor of violence in the world." In November of 1967, King said in a speech on the Domestic Impact of the War, "The government is emotionally committed to the war. It is emotionally hostile to the needs of the poor." During his last formal sermon at the Washington National Cathedral, he called Vietnam "one of the most unjust wars that has ever been fought in the history

---

[2] Senator Church's Committee on Intelligence Overreach found that Hoover and the FBI illegally spied on innocent citizens incorrectly targeted as insurgents between 1960 and 1974. The committee did not have access to evidence that such activity occurred for a longer period.

of the world," and elaborated: "It has strengthened the military-industrial complex; it has strengthened the forces of reaction in our nation . . . and put us in the position of protecting a corrupt regime that is stacked against the poor." As these statements demonstrate, King's campaign addressed more than racial injustice. Unfortunately, the issue of poverty presented a means by which he gained additional opponents, particularly large business owners. Some of the reformations he wanted were higher wages, reasonable health care and safe working conditions, which, if implemented, would have re-distributed some of the wealth of powerful economic forces to their workers. King's last effort to address the problems of the lower class was the Poor People's Campaign, a multi-racial protest of impoverished people who would camp out in close proximity to the White House until the government agreed to pass progressive economic legislation. His assassination occurred about a month before that was scheduled to occur.

Chapter 2
Big Brother Cracks Down on Thought Crimes

Senator Church's Committee on Intelligence Overreach in the mid-1970s revealed that on April 4th, 1964 FBI headquarters detailed various means of defaming King and members of his organization, including "possibilities of anonymous source contacts, possibilities of utilizing contacts in the news media field; initiating discreet checks relative to developing background information on employees of [King's organization] the Southern Christian Leadership Conference [SCLC]. . . ." The same committee found that the FBI had used their employees and the media to convince the public that Dr. King secretly conspired to promote violence and communism.

One example of propaganda appeared in the *Augusta Courier* in 1963. The newspaper displayed a photograph of King at the Highlander Folk School in Tennessee, an institution that focused on educating adults about racial and economic issues. Yet the anonymous writer referred to it as a "Communist Training School." In the photograph, King sits beside three men whose associations with the Communist Party are grossly exaggerated in the accompanying article. The media claims about the Highlander Folk School have since been discredited, yet the same article is still finding readers today on a white supremacist website that encourages students to download slanderous flyers about the civil rights leader and distribute them at school.

William Schaap, a specialist in military law who taught propaganda courses at John Jay College and wrote various narratives on intelligence-related matters, summarized the relatively unknown findings of the Church Committee and other congressional reports while testifying as an expert witness during *King v. Jowers and Other Unknown Co-Conspirators*.

Schaap spoke of the Crime Reporting Division at the FBI, the department responsible for developing favorable partners in the media and keeping track of journalists that exposed government corruption. ". . . The Church Committee report gives . . . many, many examples - copies of memos from [FBI director, J. Edgar] Hoover on down where there would be a thing attached and say, get this information to our friends at the *Copley News Service*, get this to our friends at *Reader's Digest*, get this to our friendly A.P. reporter and so on. And then, of course, they would show the clipping indicating that in fact someone had gotten it to their friends, and it would then go over the wires or appear in stories." Schaap referred to Hoover also working with *U.S. News and World Report* as well as "friendly reporters in Memphis," where King's assassination occurred.

The FBI initiated a Counterintelligence Program (COINTELPRO) to oppose threats to the American republic. "And it was," said Schaap, "at least in my opinion, rather paranoid in what it considered threats. It had divisions trying to operate against communists, against socialists, against the New Left, against the Old Left, against what they referred to as Black Nationalists, what they referred to as hate groups. They had a separate section just on the Nation of Islam. They had a separate section on the Civil Rights Movement . . . what counter intelligence programs were, were overt attempts - sometimes very, very complicated operations to disrupt organizations which they felt were a threat regardless of whether the organizations were committing any crimes . . . it basically took the position that, you know, thinking bad thoughts was a crime. Or if you didn't like the current government of the day, that was a crime. And if J. Edgar

Hoover decided the group should be disrupted, then COINTELPRO would sit down and figure out how to disrupt it."

Consequently, when King scheduled peaceful marches, the "danger in demonstrations" became a media focus and newspaper artist depictions portrayed him as angry and malicious, expressions absent in reality.

The CIA became involved as well, implementing Operation Chaos to target "Black Nationalists" through various media sources.[3]

---

[3] Pulitzer Prize winning journalist Carl Bernstein has written about the relationship between the CIA and the media. He implicated Henry Luce of *Time Magazine,* as well as *CBS,* the *New York Times,* the *Copley News Service, ABC, NBC,* the *Associated Press, United Press International, Reuters, Hearst Newspapers, Scripps-Howard, Newsweek Magazine,* and the *Mutual Broadcasting System,* as among those that have performed propaganda services for the CIA. Bernstein says that since 1973, the CIA "has cut back sharply on the use of reporters . . ."

Government agencies do not publicly discuss which media outlets they use to promote propaganda today.

Chapter 3
The Suicide Letter

In 1963, Attorney General Robert Kennedy learned that one of King's speechwriters, Stanley Levison, had been a former member of the Communist Party. He then authorized the FBI to wiretap and watch the civil rights leader.[4] Agents planted electronic bugs and covertly infiltrated King's Southern Christian Leadership Conference (SCLC). Intensive investigation revealed that King had unknowingly received donated blood from a communist after being stabbed, and that another member of the SCLC, Jack O'Dell, once belonged to the Communist Party but had since severed ties. Despite associations too feeble to be incriminating, Hoover and his FBI refused to relent.

One year later, Dr. King received a package that contained a letter crafted to appear written by a disgruntled citizen. Senator Church's Committee on intelligence Overreach confirmed that FBI agent William C. Sullivan, presumably operating under orders from

---

[4] Asked in 1964 about the nature of Hoover's character, Robert Kennedy replied, "I think he's dangerous." Referring to Hoover, Kennedy also told one of his speechwriters John Bartlow Martin, "He's rather a psycho . . . it's a very dangerous organization . . . and I think he's . . . become senile and rather . . . frightening."

Hoover, wrote it. The package of hate mail also included audio recordings, allegedly of King engaging in extramarital sexual relations.

For years, portions of the long-winded, grammatically dismal letter were redacted, but in 2014, Yale Professor Beverly Gage found an uncensored version in the National Archives. Aside from discriminating terminology describing King as an "evil, abnormal beast," the letter asserted that infidelity made King an ungodly, confused, and harmful man. After repeatedly stating, "You are done," the cryptic message in the last paragraph is, "There is only one thing left for you to do. You know what it is. . . . There is but one way out for you. You better take it before your filthy, abnormal fraudulent self is bared to the nation." King and his advisors perceived this as a suggestion to commit suicide and most scholars agree with that interpretation. Having investigated King exhaustively, the FBI must have been aware that the subject of their attention had, at age twelve, jumped from a window in the second story of his home after his grandmother died. Furthermore, if the FBI simply intended to suggest that King should resign from his civil-rights campaign, they could have clearly stated that without fabricating a letter.

Although writers have focused on the proposition to commit suicide, little has been said about the repeated statement "you are done." It is difficult to read those words without interpreting them as a threat.

King received repeated death threats during his campaign for peace. He endured assault, stabbing, incarceration; on one occasion segregationists firebombed his house. "This is what will happen to me," he remarked after viewing John F. Kennedy's assassination on television. Occasionally, he felt discouraged. It would have been safe to fade out of the public eye. Alternatively, he could have summoned the strength of the masses fed up with inequality, taken a gun himself, and fought tyranny in the violent manner of most wars. Such a strategy would have been decidedly simpler than persistent attempts to promote peace. However, despite colossal adversity, he never gave up on civil disobedience. He persisted under the belief that his cause remained more important than his life. Such a noble choice places him in an exclusive group of historical heroes that have been willing to die for justice alongside those suffering on the front lines of adversity, in contrast to the many political authorities that have not been interested in fighting hand in hand with the men and women sent to war.

Chapter 4
James Earl Ray

The "summer of love" may have been mislabeled. Although many Americans embraced peace and unity in 1967, race riots and anti-war protests raged from Washington D.C. to San Francisco. The New York State Athletic Commission withdrew Muhammad Ali's WBA title after he refused military service in Vietnam. As Jimi Hendrix sang "We're all bold as love," George Wallace was preaching from a platform of prejudice and drumming up considerable support as a presidential candidate.

On April 23 of that year, a man named James Earl Ray was in the midst of a serving a twenty year robbery sentence at Missouri State Penitentiary. He arrived customarily at the prison bakery for work that day, but then proceeded to squeeze himself into an industrial-sized breadbox. An accomplice covered him with a partition and placed loaves of bread atop it. Ray was then loaded onto a truck, probably with more inside help, considering that the breadbox he inhabited must have weighed substantially more than the others.

Exactly how he got out of the truck beyond the prison grounds is unclear. Some report that he wriggled out of the box and jumped out the back.

Similarly, the details and timeframe of Ray's exact whereabouts after that are fuzzy due to differing accounts. However, sources place Ray in Montreal and Toronto within two months of his escape. He likely then spent time in Birmingham, Alabama. After that, he travelled to Mexico, drank heavily and patronized prostitutes while masquerading as a pornography director, according to the author Hampton Sides, who also detailed Ray subsequently settling in Los Angeles, getting a nose job, taking dancing lessons, and registering for courses in bartending and locksmithing.

In the course of this activity, Ray certainly did not plan to become an international fugitive, nor an infamous controversial figure for the remainder of his life.

Chapter 5
Memphis Sanitation Workers Strike

Dr. King's "I Have a Dream" speech, delivered on the steps of the Lincoln Memorial in 1963, heralded the Civil Rights Act (1964) and the Voting Rights Act (1965). Nevertheless, legislation does not necessarily alleviate the destructive maladies of discrimination and greed. As written in *Strength to Love,* a collection of King's sermons, "Morality cannot be legislated, but behavior can be regulated. Judicial decrees cannot change the heart but they can restrain the heartless." Accordingly, although King fostered societal progress in the 1960s, racism, wealth inequality and worker rights remained largely neglected issues.

Consequently, by 1967 King had devised a plan to march a large group of Americans to Washington D.C. for the purpose of staging protests and badgering politicians until the government agreed to implement comprehensive social reform. Unemployment, education, and a reasonable minimum wage included King's concerns.

Before the Poor People's Campaign, however, a simmering situation in a southern city caught King's attention. University of Washington professor and author Michael Honey describes, in his *Going Down Jericho Road,* the dismal conditions black garbage workers in Memphis endured under the mayorship of Henry Loeb in 1968.

Loeb ignored repeated pleas to replace dangerously dysfunctional trucks and refused to compensate black employees that were forced to work overtime. Demeaning, white supervisors in the sanitation department, who referred to elderly black men as "boy," received pay when it rained, yet sent black employees home with only two hours pay. No union or any other mechanism existed to protect workers who consistently operated in hazardous conditions and occasionally complained of being short-changed. In addition, low wages left workers without the money required to buy enough food for their families.

In contrast, Mayor Loeb and his family prospered from real estate investments and the ownership of numerous businesses, including laundromats and barbeque restaurants. The low wages Loeb paid to black employees at the many businesses he owned in town undoubtedly augmented his wealth.

On February 1, 1968, two sanitation workers were crushed to death by a defective truck that had been inadequately repaired after killing two men in 1964. Eleven days later, more than a thousand members of the Memphis Department of Public Works went on strike. On February 22, the City Council proposed a wage increase and voted to acknowledge a workers' union. Loeb overruled them. The next day, Memphis Police maced and tear-gassed nonviolent protestors marching to city hall.

In response to the incident, Loeb chose to adopt an authoritarian attitude of paternal infantilization. News footage captured the mayor's stance: "Public employees cannot strike against their employer and this you cannot do. I suggested to these men today that they go back to work. . . . As long as you continue to break the law and continue to break the law, there will be no talks at any level of government." He likely would have disregarded the significance of words King wrote from a Birmingham jail in 1963: "We should never forget that everything Adolf Hitler did in Germany was legal." While the Constitution affirms the right to assembly on a federal level, specific state laws and the withholding of a permits has legally deterred peaceful protests.

A prominent local minister and community organizer, James Lawson, asked Dr. King to join him in Memphis to promote the workers' cause. Ralph Abernathy and Andrew Young, two men close to King and high-ranking members of the SCLC, expressed fears of a setup and other possible dangers. Memphis hosted a famous annual cotton carnival that culminated in the symbolic royal crowning of prominent white family members. The spectacle praised the prosperity slavery had brought some of the families that still owned businesses in town. Loeb's wife, Mary Gregg, had actually been crowned cotton queen in 1950, and her ancestors had owned slaves. In addition, a local newspaper, *The Commercial Appeal*, featured a popular prejudiced comic called *Hambone's Meditations*. To top it all off, the Police and Fire Director in Memphis, Frank Holloman, formerly belonged to the FBI and had worked closely with King's adversary, J. Edgar Hoover. Yet King refused to back down from the perils Memphis presented, and insisted on leading a peaceful march in the southern city. He had already been receiving regular death threats.

On March 28, a riot broke out during the protest. Despite their efforts, King and his entourage failed to prevent police and frustrated young men from clashing. During the chaos, a local officer escorted King away to a hotel. Stores in Downtown Memphis were looted; a teenage black boy, Larry Payne, "witnesses said, had his hands in the air when a police officer stuck a shotgun in his stomach and pulled the trigger," wrote Michael Honey.

At one point during the chaos, James Lawson and other ministers engaged in a series of phone calls with Frank Holloman in an effort to resolve the conflict, to no avail. When protestors retreated to a church called Clayborn Temple, police followed them. Those who tried to exit were pushed back with clubs and tear gas. Young men, taking a stand outside, retaliated by throwing bricks at officers, who, in turn, entered the church and proceeded to beat and gas innocent people attempting to hide from the violence. Although the media painted black men as inflammatory, the public never learned exactly who instigated the conflict.[5] Payne suffered the only fatality while police injured numerous black citizens that wanted nothing to do with the conflict. "It was a police attack on the movement," explained Honey in an interview.

Military intelligence expert William Schapp spoke of the FBI's use of the media against King before and after the Memphis march. "The campaign against Dr. King's activities went up to the very last day of his life. In particular, on his involvement with the strike in Memphis, the FBI decided at that point to try to spread stories that he was encouraging violence. One of the key articles was in the *Christian Science Monitor* at the end of March of '68 and, again, gives all of the themes that the FBI wanted planted, particularly about violence. . . . And this story refers to it [the sanitation strike] as a potentially cataclysmic racial confrontation. Not quite World War III, but along that kind of language. And stories that began to appear—and this was just before Dr. King was killed—were suggesting that he was closely allied with violent forces." Schapp referred to such articles displayed during *King v. Jowers and Other Unknown Co-Conspirators*.

---

[5] Possible suspects include an undercover agent, one or many policemen, officer and FBI informant Darrell McCullough, a member of the Invaders, and a local teenager.

Chapter 6
A Tragedy of Kings

Dr. King decided to schedule another march in Memphis on April 8, which he hoped would correct what had gone wrong.

Meanwhile, leaders of a black rights group, "The Invaders," visited King. They warned him of an assassination conspiracy and expressed shock that he had no security. "If someone really wants to kill me," King replied, "there's nothing I can do about it." Ralph Abernathy, successive president of the SCLC, later said he believed that King "had received, through letter or telephone, some knowledge that something was going to happen . . . some word or some source that he was going to be assassinated." King had repeatedly referred to the probability and so had his wife, Coretta. The "suicide letter" from the FBI may have been one such indication.

On April 4, 1968, Dr. King resided in room 306 at the Lorraine Motel in Memphis. The Invaders had also checked into the Lorraine, with a considerable number of weapons, which they considered necessary to defend themselves and King from local police and a potential assassin. They met with the SCLC that day and requested a large sum of money in exchange for their service as peacekeepers during the imminent march. Soon after the meeting, they were told by an employee that the SCLC would no longer pay for their stay.[6] Ultimately, the Invaders, and their security presence, left at least eleven minutes before the shooting.

A Memphis Police officer, Ed Redditt, testified during *King v. Jowers* . . . that on April 3, 1968, after escorting King from the airport, he "noticed something that was unusual." The Inspector in charge of security, Don Smith, was ordering him to leave, but "there was nobody else there" to provide a guard in Redditt's absence. In previous visits, Redditt and his partner Willie Richmond had been assigned to tail and spy on King. Their responsibilities included writing down license plate numbers and attempting to identify the people with whom King associated, which had required them to stay close to the civil rights leader. The order confused Redditt, so he went to the fire station across the street and asked if he could watch from there.

Two hours before King's assassination on the evening of April 4, Redditt was back watching the Lorraine Motel from Fire Station No. 2 when Memphis Police Intelligence Lieutenant Eli Arkin arrived to escort him into a conference room at police headquarters. Officers and others whom Redditt did not recognize filled the room. Director Frank Holloman told Redditt that there was a contract on his life. "He knew as well as I that you couldn't stop a contract," Redditt testified. Nevertheless, Holloman made sure that Arkin accompanied Redditt home.

A record of Redditt's statement to the Memphis police on April 10, 1968 indicates that he received a death threat at the airport on April 3, and another one via a phone call to the firehouse on April 4. Redditt described these threats as "part of a policeman's job." When asked, "Did you take them seriously?" he replied, "Not really. If you do, you need to resign. That's the way I felt. . . . Nothing unusual."

---

[6] Reports indicate that King was offended by attempted extortion and initiated the removal of the Invaders from the Lorraine Motel. Invaders co-founder Charles Cabbage later recalled that he received a phone call from the front desk and was informed that Jesse Jackson said the SCLC would no longer pay their bill.

After Redditt's removal, his partner, Willie Richmond, remained at the firehouse to conduct surveillance, contrary to traditional protocol. Said Redditt: "I had a doubt about my partner in the first place. It is unusual getting somebody that you don't know anything about to be assigned to you. Number two, in that day there was two men always worked together. Whatever happened to one man would happen to the other. So if you got a threat, both partners got a threat. I always wondered what happened to him, why wasn't he removed, why wasn't he taken a long with me. I never got that answer."

Through slits cut into newspaper taped to the locker room rear door window, Richmond continued to peer across Mulberry Street and slightly to the north (his left) at the Lorraine Motel. A parking area with bushes in front of it sat to his left, beside the firehouse. The brush extended further to the north and up a slope, deeper into a lot that housed two buildings. The closest building to the firehouse contained the south wing of a rooming house and a business called Canipe's Amusement Company. The building on the other side of that included the restaurant Jim's Grill beneath the north wing of the rooming house in which James Earl Ray resided that day.

During his vigil, Richmond observed a handsome, confident black man. Unfettered by the chains of subservience, Dr. King stood on the balcony of the hotel, near his room, 306, jovially bantering with his chauffer and colleagues in the parking lot below.

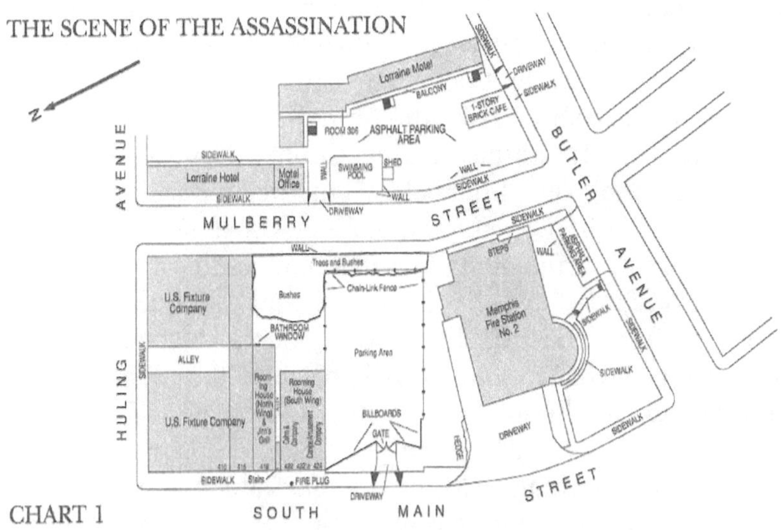

A firefighter named George Loenneke met Richmond at his post. According to testimony from Richmond as well as statements taken by the Memphis PD and the FBI, when Richmond allowed Loenneke a peek through the binoculars at 6:01 p.m., the assassin shot King.

Between 5:45 and 6:10, James Earl Ray exited the rooming house onto South Main Street, located on the side of the building that faced away from the Lorraine and Mulberry Street. According to the FBI, he left a bundle that included a rifle, ammunition, binoculars, and a radio in the visible entryway of Canipe's Amusement Company after the shooting at 6:01. However, the lawyer, Arthur Hanes Jr. testified in 1999 that the owner of Canipe's said the bundle was dropped off ten minutes before the shooting. Why a guilty man would leave a package with the murder weapon in plain view immediately after committing a crime is hard to fathom, perhaps unless he was working with someone who told him to do so. Since no motive beyond the possible promise of payment has been established for Ray, such a discrepancy remains worthy of examination.

Additional unanswered questions abound. Considering that death threats are an inherent part of working for the police department, why was Redditt removed? He was later told that the contract had been on someone else. Is it just a coincidence that the one moment during a long surveillance assignment when Officer Richmond relinquished his view to Loenneke happened to coincide with the moment King was shot? After his initial short statement, available, albeit blurred, at the online Shelby County Register of Deeds, no new information on Loenneke emerged during the HSCA investigation, and he was not available or chose not to testify during *King v. Jowers* . . . . Incidentally, video and audio of James Earl Ray in custody, recorded by the Shelby County Police later in 1968 (released in 2013), contains distorted segments. A statement from the Shelby County website claims this is because the men operating the machinery did not know how to use it properly. Why were four tactical police units patrolling the vicinity of the Lorraine withdrawn just before the shooting? (More on that later.) Police in uniform arrived on the scene one to two minutes after the crime, but failed to apprehend an assassin who could not have been far away. "There were 40 police cars roaming the downtown and central portions of Memphis," Michael Honey explained in an interview. "There were FBI [agents] posted around the Lorraine Motel. The Military Intelligence Division of the U.S. Army had operatives in the city. So you had all these law enforcement and paramilitary agents operating, and yet, this one person—supposedly James Earl Ray—was able to penetrate all of that, shoot King, and get away."

Ray's fingerprints were found on the rifle and other items in the bundle, but not in the rooming house bathroom, where authorities alleged the shot was taken. In addition, investigators apparently did not check the bathroom window for gunpowder residue, which would have confirmed the source of the shot. Investigators never adequately linked the bullet that killed King to the rifle with Ray's fingerprints, nor did they prove Ray was ever in the bathroom. Who first discovered the bundle is also unclear. The state initially claimed that Memphis Police Homicide Chief N.E. Zachary arrived first on the scene. Zachary denied it and the state responded that it had actually been Bud Ghormley. Then, Deputy Vernon Dollahite contradicted that with a statement that *he* had been the first law enforcement official to find the bundle. Such inconsistencies have cast doubt on the reliability of the investigations conducted by the FBI and the Memphis Police.

The United States lost a hero and true champion of the people at 7:05 PM when Dr. Martin Luther King, Jr. passed away. Accounts describe cheering when FBI headquarters in King's hometown of Atlanta received the news. According to an article in the Chicago Reader by documentarians John Sergeant and John Edginton, FBI agent Arthur Murtaugh said his colleague "leapt up, clapped his hands, and said, 'Goddamn, we got him! We finally got him.'" According to subsequent sources, including Hampton Sides, however, the colleague's statement was, "They got Zorro! [King's FBI code name] Thank God, they finally got the S.O.B." Cheering the death of a good man certainly exemplifies a sort of maliciousness that is disturbing to consider among authorities whose responsibilities include protecting Americans. Also noteworthy, however, is that the "we" in "we got him" was later quoted as "they." Despite the fact that a large portion of FBI resources had been dedicated to "neutralizing" King, it is not apparent how exactly that quote changed.

After the shooting, back in Memphis, a man speaking over a CB radio transmission claimed to be chasing down the suspect car, a white Ford Mustang. The experienced Police and Fire Director Frank Holloman, who had previously worked with Hoover for the FBI, did not stop his officers from pursuing the lead of this apparently unknown person who avoided disclosing his name. When the driver abruptly ceased communications over the radio, it became obvious that a diversion had taken place. The police had only set up roadblocks on Summer Avenue, where the driver claimed to be following the suspect. The main routes out of the city had been left open, possibly allowing the assassin to escape. Neither authorities nor investigators have publicly confirmed the identity of the voice behind the hoax.

Holloman expressed extreme efforts by his department to find the "person or persons responsible," and stated, "From the evidence we have at this time, only one man was involved." In addition, Holloman claimed not to have had "a scintilla or an iota of a desire to see any harm come to Dr. King," and described the tragedy as "one of the greatest disappointments in my life." Whether one chooses to believe if Holloman had a "scintilla" or an "iota" of malice toward King, he did allow his officers to commit violent acts against peaceful black protestors repeatedly.

Chapter 7
Ripples of a Dream

Dr. King's passing touched people all over the world. Indira Gandhi called it "a setback to mankind's search for light." Moscow Radio referred to King as a "man of crystal purity, straight and incorruptible," and proclaimed "another dark page of crime has been written in the United States."

A Senator of South Carolina, Strom Thurmond, said, "I hesitate to say anything bad about the dead, but I do not share a high regard for Dr. King. He only pretended to be non-violent." John Connally, a governor from Texas, asserted that King "contributed much to the chaos and turbulence in this country." Presidential hopeful George Wallace was not available for comment but the chairman of his campaign, Bob Walters, said, "Although he claimed to be a non-violent man, he spread the seeds of violence which are now in the country. You shall reap what you sow."

The irony of segregationists calling a pacifist violent might be laughable if the tactics that cause people believe such falsehood were not so tragic. The words of Thurmond, Connally and Walters exemplify a common *tu quoque* method of deception, in which one who operates with questionable ethics accuses an opponent of the same depravity in an effort to re-direct the blame from himself. In-depth examination of the situation reveals that King preached, practiced and promoted non-violence throughout his campaign.

Said King: "Like an unchecked cancer, hate corrodes the personality and eats away its vital unity. Hate destroys a man's sense of values and his objectivity. It causes him to describe the beautiful as ugly and the ugly as beautiful, and to confuse the true with the false and the false with the true."

In a conversation with SCLC member Andrew Young, Dr. King's seven-year-old son Dexter said, "This man didn't know our daddy, did he? . . . Because if he had, he wouldn't have shot him. He was just an ignorant man who didn't know any better." It was the FBI's persistent propaganda campaign that, at least in part, accounted for the results of a Gallup poll conducted in 1966, which revealed that only 33% of Americans had positive feelings toward Dr. King. Activist and humanitarian, Benjamin Elijah Mays said, ". . . make no mistake, the American people are in part responsible. The assassin heard enough condemnation of King and of Negroes to feel that he had public support." Unfortunately, many personal perspectives of King were molded by prejudiced traditions, authorities and the media. Independent analysis would have facilitated a more realistic view.

Attorney General Ramsey Clark, an outward proponent of civil rights, described the assassination as "a tragic setback . . ." Yet he also said that one man was likely responsible early in the investigation, at a time when he could not have known that for sure. Then he put the FBI, who he knew had attacked King for years, in charge of the manhunt, apparently because he thought it was the only agency with the appropriate resources.

According to Hampton Sides, Cartha DeLoach, assistant director of the FBI, said that Hoover was "as anxious as anyone to find King's killer, even though he disapproved of the man. We had a job to do and we were prepared to do it. The case was handled in a very intensified manner, and everyone in the FBI was called upon to help out." Yet DeLoach, who led the FBI's investigation, had been Hoover's accomplice in slandering King. In addition, that particular statement from DeLoach is consistent with media reports intended to boost the FBI's image amid public understanding of Hoover's animosity toward King. William Schapp explained: "Drew Pearson, who was a very close friend of Hoover's, had a nationally syndicated column and wrote one basically designed to try and kill the rumors that Hoover wasn't trying hard because he didn't like King. And in it Pearson says he is convinced that the FBI is conducting perhaps the most painstaking exhaustive manhunt ever before undertaken in the United States. Why - how he would know is beyond us, but that's clearly what Hoover told him to say. . . . But they also had another one of their very close operatives, Jeremiah O'Leary, who was then with the *Washington Star*, did an article for the *Reader's Digest*. And he went one beyond Pearson and said it was the greatest manhunt in law enforcement history in the world. So he was now saying this wasn't only the greatest manhunt in America, it was the greatest manhunt ever, anywhere."

After reading a telegram from Dr. King's father that stressed the importance of carrying on the legacy of non-violence, President Johnson said in a meeting with civil rights leaders, "If I were a kid in Harlem, I know what I'd be thinking. I'd be thinking that whites had declared open season on my people - that they're going to pick us off one by one unless I get a gun and pick them off first." The empathy in his words, however, was somewhat tarnished by his decision not to attend King's funeral on April 9.

As fires and riots sprouted in various cities including Washington D.C., the National Guard arrived in Memphis with helicopters and tanks. No officers or white people suffered fatalities in Memphis during the anger and confusion following the assassination, however, a black citizen named Ellis Tate was shot nine times and killed by police. Witnesses said that Tate had his hands in the air when an officer first pulled the trigger and the explanation from the Memphis police regarding the incident changed in the course of several days.

In a radio broadcast, James Lawson urged the black community to exhibit restraint. "What did you expect?" Lyndon Johnson stated. ". . . When you put your foot on a man's neck and hold him down for three hundred years, and then you let him up, what's he going to do? He's going to knock your block off." However, the president was wrong about that. The black community overwhelmingly chose not to kill white people in retaliation, even after years of atrocious hate crimes and the murder of every impoverished citizen's hope for a better life.

Referring to frightened young police preparing for a violent race war, Johnson later told a staffer, "I'm not getting through to them. They're holed up like generals in a dugout, getting ready to watch a war."

Memphis Mayor Henry Loeb was no exception. Even as he went on television urging the community to "maintain peace and honor" in the tradition of King, he had a loaded shotgun in the foot well of his desk.

Outside the mayor's building, sanitation workers marched with signs that read "I Am a Man," a slogan not so different from "Black Lives Matter," the recent response to police killings of unarmed black men across the United States. A Justice Department official, Roger Wilkins, said of Loeb, "he did not have one inch of sympathy for these men and women who were out there pacing around the building." Loeb had repeatedly refused basic human rights to black workers. He supported segregation and built on his millions by refusing to pay living wages, while his employees struggled to feed themselves. Such an attitude encouraged the idea that black citizens were irrelevant and compounded the racial conflict in Memphis.

As tensions surged, Loeb experienced pressure from powerful political players including Ramsey Clark to resolve the strike. Ultimately, the union undermined the mayor, negotiating directly with the City Council, and Loeb was compelled to concede. Finally, the workers received union recognition, the automatic deduction of union dues, a more lucid grievance procedure, and ten cents per hour raises.

Loeb was not personally interested in financially contributing to the workers' cause and there was nothing in the Memphis budget, yet an industrialist, Abe Plough, stepped up and donated sixty thousand dollars. Plough had built a fortune after being born poor, which may have enabled him to empathize with the needs of the less wealthy. Nevertheless, his role in resolving this dispute exemplifies behavior that has a positive cultural impact, and his financial success proves that an intelligent person can get rich and support social reform simultaneously.

Chapter 8
The Investigation

Captain Jewell Ray of the Memphis Police Intelligence Department led the initial local investigation. After observing the package left at the amusement shop, he interviewed two men, Willie Anschutz and Charlie Stephens, who had shared the rooming house with James Earl Ray. They said that on the evening of April 4, the new tenant had been occupying the bathroom for a long period. Then they heard a gunshot, and then a man carrying a bundle walked past them in the hallway. Stephens, an alcoholic war veteran, was highly intoxicated the day he made that statement, and nobody else in the rooming house besides Anschutz corroborated it, yet it became the foundation upon which the case against James Ray sits. When Stephens was shown a photograph of Ray during a later interview on CBS, he said that the man in the picture did not match who he had seen.

Of the numerous fingerprints on the rifle and binoculars that had been left in the doorway of the amusement shop, two matching prints turned out to be those of Eric Starvo Galt, according to the FBI. "Galt" had registered his name and vehicle details at the New Rebel Motel in Memphis on April 3, before re-locating to the rooming house across the street from the Lorraine on April 4. It would later be revealed that "Galt" was one of the aliases that James Earl Ray adopted, in addition to "John Willard," "Harvey Lowmeyer," and "Ramon George Sneyd."

As the investigation continued, the Chief of the Firearms Identification Unit at the FBI, Robert A. Frazier, said the bullet that killed King could have come from the Gamemaster rifle, which they had learned "Galt" recently purchased, but he could not rule out that it might have been fired from a different rifle because the impact mangled the soft round bullet, leaving it devoid of revealing characteristics. A forensic expert testified during a 1974 hearing that the bullet was initially relatively intact until the FBI handled it. Frazier also determined that the bathroom window of the rooming house had an indentation that could have resulted from firing a Gamemaster rifle, but again, he could not say so definitively. Since no "partially burned or unburned gunpowder" remained on King's clothes, the shot was not taken from close range.

According to the FBI, James Earl Ray drove from Memphis to Atlanta during the night of April 4, 1968. Although police and the FBI were looking for a white Mustang, none of them noticed it driving four hundred miles through Mississippi and Alabama during a manhunt. After making his way to Detroit, Ray took a taxi through the Windsor Tunnel and crossed into Canada on Saturday, April 6. That same day in Oakland, police ambushed a car filled with Black Panther Party members, a shootout followed, and a teenage black boy, Bobby Hutton, was shot twelve times after he had surrendered and stripped down to his underwear to prove he was unarmed. Meanwhile, J. Edgar Hoover was in Baltimore, enjoying a customary weekend of horseracing.

On April 8, King's widow, Coretta returned to lead the second Memphis march. Members of the National Guard secured the route while Police Director Frank Holloman and casually dressed law enforcement officials on Harley Davidsons proceeded a short distance before the King family and 20,000 citizens from across the country. Although riots had been occurring in a hundred thirty-five American cities, peace prevailed in Memphis that day.

In Toronto, Ray acquired a passport that named him Ramon George Sneya. According to the FBI and some writers that support the "lone-wolf" theory, it was not difficult to obtain a fraudulent Canadian passport and the manager of a travel agency helped Ray fill out the paperwork. However, a man named Jules "Ricco" Kimble, who claimed to have worked for the CIA, said in a 1989 interview from prison that he flew James Ray to Montreal in July of 1967. According to Kimble, that was when a CIA specialist provided Ray with an identities packet, which likely contained fraudulent passports, aliases, and information on how to deceive people by altering one's image. This claim and comprehensive evidence that Ray did spend time in Montreal within months of his prison escape on April 23, 1967 has initiated the possibility that Ray already had the fraudulent passport or that the CIA helped Ray obtain it in 1968. Conversely, government investigators have said that Ray acted alone in establishing the multiple identities he adopted.

The aliases Ray used were not fabricated. Each identity was stolen from real men with physical similarities to him. Many journalists have considered it highly improbable that Ray would have been able to find such suitable candidates and conduct his nefarious activities alone while on the run.

The FBI kept most of the details of the investigation to themselves until April 17, when they issued a statement that they were looking for a man named Eric Starvo Galt, who operated under two aliases, John Willard and Harvey Lowmeyer. He was uneducated, a drinker, a dancer, a listener of country and western music, armed and dangerous, and he had taken part in a conspiracy, probably with his brother, "to injure, oppress, threaten, or intimidate Martin Luther King, Junior." Along with this statement, the FBI released two versions of a bartending school graduation picture, one in which "Galt" had his eyes closed, and another, doctored somewhat inaccurately by an artist to portray him with eyes open.

Two days later, the FBI declared that the fingerprints they previously said belonged to "Eric Galt" actually matched James Earl Ray, who had escaped from the state penitentiary in Jefferson City, Missouri the previous year. Wanted notices went out across the nation, and in Mexico but not Canada. The public learned that Ray was a high school dropout who had served briefly in the army before being discharged because of "ineptness and lack of adaptability for military service." He had committed crimes of burglary, forgery, and armed robbery, often in a bungling manner, and he had served a few jail sentences. Neither murder nor manslaughter were among his convictions. In prison, he had earned a reputation for being cunning in scheming ways, but perhaps he had more gall than intelligence, exemplified by his repeated mistakes, including one occasion on which he fell out of his own getaway car because he forgot to close the door.

James's brother, John, managed a bar in St. Louis called the Grapevine Tavern, a popular haven for segregationists. The FBI initially claimed to believe that John was part of the assassination conspiracy but they were never able to establish a plausible link.

When Jerry Ray, another sibling, was asked about James's involvement, he said, "He wouldn't have put himself in a spot like this unless there was something in it for him."

Chapter 9
The Poor People's Campaign

Determined to maintain King's dream, Reverend Ralph Abernathy, the new president of the SCLC, secured a permit from the National Park Service for the previously scheduled Poor People's Campaign to commence on May 12 in West Potomac Park beside the mall in Washington D.C.

Citizens of various ancestry comprised the thousands of demonstrators who set up tents in what was labeled Resurrection City. The attendance was considerably lower than the SCLC had hoped, probably because the media had fostered fear of a race war and impoverished citizens did not have the luxury of being able to take time away from work. Accounts of the actual number vary considerably, from 2,000 to 7,000 people.

Under the backdrop of parades and live music, Ralph Abernathy unveiled his plans to create a guaranteed annual minimum wage, to solve hunger in the United States, and to improve urban ghettos.

The resources of the FBI were redirected from tracking down King's assassin to spying on the marchers and defending Washington from what some authorities saw as an assault. Said Attorney General Ramsey Clark: "There were predictions of holocaust, and absurdly improbable testimony on the Hill about clandestine meetings and planned violence. The nation was led to expect horrible crimes." Senator John McClellan of Arkansas, for example, claimed he had intelligence that black militants were planning a coup d'état. Such evidence never surfaced. Incidentally, many politicians must have realized that their failure to address domestic poverty was exactly what had created a Poor People's Campaign to begin with.

Ralph Abernathy and the leaders of the Poor People's Campaign continually encouraged peaceful behavior, not only verbally, but in action as well. Therefore, the idea that protestors would resort to large-scale violence in Washington was unlikely, but that did not stop the media from fostering foreboding possibilities. Subsequently, white people inclined to discriminate must have felt legitimized by reports that depicted black citizens as dangerous or violent.

J. Edgar Hoover wrote a memo to his informants, encouraging them to "document such things as immorality, indecency, dishonesty, and hypocrisy" entertained by the leaders of the SCLC during the protest. Although a few conflicts among non-SCLC demonstrators, police, and an escaped mental patient are reported to have occurred, there were no fatalities or serious injuries.

As the month of May progressed, frequent rain turned the park into a muddy mess. On June 5, Senator Robert Kennedy, the only presidential candidate who had openly backed the Poor People's Campaign, was shot to death in a Los Angeles hotel. He was the fourth influential American equal rights proponent to be assassinated in a five year period.[7] As the funeral procession passed through Resurrection City, demonstrators somberly watched their hopes dwindle.

The park permit expired on June 23, 1968. The next day, police cleared the area of protestors and arrested those not interested in leaving, effectively putting an end to the Poor People's Campaign. Ultimately, the demonstration created a measure of awareness, however, it was unsuccessful in convincing Washington to solve the problems of poverty.

---

[7] John Kennedy (1963), Malcolm X (1965), Martin Luther King, Jr. (1968), Robert Kennedy (1968). Nelson Mandela was issued a long term prison sentence in 1964.

In an effort to explain the fear among authorities regarding the protest, Ramsey Clark revealed a measure of truth and a misconception: ". . . poverty is miserable," he wrote. "It is ugly, disorganized, rowdy, sick, uneducated, violent, afflicted with crime. Poverty demeans human dignity. The demanding tone, the inarticulateness, the implied violence deeply offended us. We didn't want to see it on our sacred monumental grounds. We wanted it out of sight and out of mind."

Perhaps activities occurring on the other side of the world were easier to keep "out of sight and out of mind." At the same time as the Poor People's Campaign, one of President Johnson's benefactors, Halliburton, was prospering from the violence in Vietnam. In addition, Dow, Monsanto, and smaller chemical companies were collaborating with the government to spray napalm and Agent Orange on Vietnamese forests, inflicting many thousands of deaths and deformities of innocent civilians, soldiers, and even unborn children, at a time when a significant number of citizens believed that the war should have been over.[8] Those types of violence, authorized in Washington, were far more widespread and destructive than anything that had occurred among impoverished attendees of any American protest.

---

[8] The destructiveness of napalm and Agent Orange remains well documented despite persistent denial by the companies involved. A substantial amount of evidence exists that Dow, Monsanto and the government knew the effects of the chemicals they were using. Admiral Elmo Zumwalt Jr., Chief of Naval Operations from 1970 to 1974, among others, brought this subject to public attention.

Chapter 10
All Crimes Matter (a Brief Interlude)

Although law enforcement and the media continue to pay a lot of attention to "street crimes" associated with poverty, examination of the types of criminals that have the most detrimental impact reveals that such attention is misplaced. Analyzing this issue is complicated, as one must ascertain exactly what sort of crimes occur on the "street" compared to those devised from a more secure setting, which can be hazy. For example, murder, assault, and theft are usually depicted as street crimes, but can also be committed by wealthy individuals. Conversely, fraud and bribery are categorized as "white-collar" although impoverished citizens, including James Earl Ray, who incidentally dressed rich, have been convicted for such violations. Corporate crime is often referred to as "white-collar," except when violence is directly involved. In addition, some of the activity that causes fatalities or negatively impacts the economy is legal, including war and the use of offshore tax havens. Therefore, something does not have to be specifically considered a crime in order for it to be harmful.

An offense analysis from the FBI's annual *Crime in the United States* indicated that, in 2014, robbery resulted in over $348 million in losses. Another "street crime," burglary, added up to nearly $3.5 billion, while larceny totaled $8.8 billion. Even if you were to quadruple the sum of those numbers in a liberal accounting for the total amount including those crimes not recognized by law enforcement, the outcome is still nowhere close to the estimated cost of white-collar crime in America, which ranges from $400 to $900 billion annually.[9]

Health care, a sector that concerned Dr. King, remains riddled with industries and personnel that compromise the general welfare of Americans. Rowan University professor of medical and economic sociology Donald W. Light collaborated with researchers at York University and Harvard Medical School in 2013 to conduct a study on the health risks of new pharmaceuticals, among other investigations. They determined that 128,000 people in the U.S. die each year from prescription drugs. In contrast, the FBI recorded slightly more than 12,000 murder offenses in 2014. Ironically, the most arrests in 2014 were violations relating to *illegal* drugs.

More notably, a study led by John Hopkins University professor of surgery and health policy Martin A. Makary, published in the *BMJ* in 2016, concluded that medical error was the third leading cause of death in the United States. This categorization is absent in reports released annually by the CDC and FBI.

The Center for Responsive Politics lists the American Medical Association as the third top spending lobbyist from 1998 to 2017.

---

[9] The 2010 National Public Survey on White-collar Crime concluded that one in four American households fell prey to white-collar crime.

    The Center for Corporate Policy: . . . " in its 2001 report the FBI estimated that the nation's total loss from robbery, burglary, larceny-theft and motor vehicle theft in 2001 was $17.2 billion—less than a third of what Enron alone cost investors, pensioners and employees that year."

    American University accounting professor and author Ralph Estes stated that, in 2000, "Americans suffered $274.7 billion dollars of damage from occupational toxic chemicals alone, along with approximately 150,000 fatalities from exposure to carcinogens in the work place. The FBI estimated that 15,517 murders occurred in 2000."

    MIT researchers from the Laboratory for Aviation and the Environment published a 2013 study that concluded an estimated "200,000 early deaths occur in the U.S. each year due to U.S. combustion emissions."

The American Hospital Association and the Pharmaceutical Research and Manufacturers were fifth and sixth respectively.

None of the aforementioned studies and reports addressed the amount of fatalities and financial damage resultant from pollution, chemicals, contaminated food, unsafe products, and stress from economic hardship, which are difficult to trace.[10]

Aside from cloaked causes of death associated with inimical behavior in the medical field, one need not dig deep to find evidence of white-collar crime in various industries.[11]

Forty corporations paid more than $100 million each in fines for environmental, and health and safety transgressions from 2010 to 2015, the Corporate Research Project revealed. BP, which sits at the top of that list, paid $25 billion during that time.

The Corporate Accountability Coalition (CAC) is comprised of a group of organizations that focus on human rights as well as corporate and environmental abuse. In 2014, the CAC determined in

---

[10] Accounting for manmade causes of cancer resultant from cumulative toxicity is challenging. A surprisingly wide array of manufactured carcinogens, ranging from alcoholic beverages to ingredients in household products, saturate modern industrial society. Pollution creates various health issues including respiratory diseases and cancer as well. Additionally, chronic stress from financial difficulty or other sources can lead to heart disease, the number one cause of death in America.

In order to definitively determine the percentage of a heart problem or cancer attributable to pollution, processed food, toxicity, stress, laziness, or unhealthy choices, a scientist would have to tediously document the lifestyles of many subjects in different environments for a lengthy period. Such a study would be expensive. While chemical proponents often argue that small doses of a toxin are safe, the companies enabled by our regulatory agencies to conduct the risk assessments on the products they sell have not been concerned with tracing *cumulative* health effects, despite short-term studies. Therefore, funding for independent analysis on the subject is necessary.

[11] Among numerous corporate criminals, Monsanto has often made headlines. In addition to settling a large lawsuit relating to the dumping of PCBs and contamination of citizens in Anniston Alabama, Monsanto was found guilty of negligence in Galveston, Texas after a worker died from leukemia resultant from exposure to benzene. Authorities in France and Brazil found Monsanto guilty of false advertising.

their annual report card that only fifteen percent of congress was concerned with holding corporations accountable, based on the issues that were supported or not. In 2016, fifty-seven percent of congress supported corporate accountability between zero and twenty-five percent of the time while only nine percent scored in the seventy-six to one hundred percent range.

Because the cost of fighting an elite financial entity in court is so high, few individuals or organizations have the means to do so. Powerful corporations can also afford superior legal representation, yet even when they are convicted, more often than not the result is a fine rather than jail time for individuals. University of Virginia Law School professor and author of *Too Big to Jail* Brandon L. Garrett examined 303 corporate cases from 2001 to 2014 and found that the justice system charged individuals only 34% of the time. Furthermore, only 42% of those convicted received a jail sentence, and most of them were low level employees, despite policies dictated by high level executives.[12]

The FBI communicated to me that white-collar crime—including those committed by corporations—is currently number seven on their list of priorities. The EPA, the IRS, the FTC, the SEC, Homeland Security and the DEA are among the numerous additional government agencies charged with investigating corporations. The inadequacy of these agencies and the failure of the mainstream media to address it can be traced to unfortunate circumstances. The fact that a handful of corporations own the media indicates that media focus points are passed down from industry superiors. A valid argument could also be made that lobbying enables corporations to own federal and state governments, including regulatory agencies.

---

[12] One example of avoidance involves a 2009 case in which the pharmaceutical company Pfizer paid $2.3 billion in fines after one of their subsidiaries pled guilty to bribing doctors, yet no senior executives suffered charges or convictions.

    The Corporate Research Project shows that major banks paid $160 billion in penalties to the Justice Department and regulatory agencies from 2010 to 2016. Stockholders frequently covered such penalties.

Conflicts of interest are worth recognizing. A rudimentary internet search exposes those who ride the revolving door back and forth between political office and industry. Fortunately, the Center for Responsive Politics traces campaign contributions, providing inquiring minds with a lead into the particular lobbying groups and corporations that have a mutually beneficial relationship with specific elected representatives. The lobbyist that spends the most to impact politics, the U.S. Chamber of Commerce, represents various corporations and industry groups and is not required to disclose their clients. However, they do list Cargill, the largest private corporation in America, as a founding member. Additional donors have included Dow Chemical Company, Monsanto, Koch Industries, Google, Microsoft, Pfizer, Merck, General Electric, Phillip Morris, Goldman Sachs, BP, and ExxonMobil.

Covert liberties that the government has taken brew additional frustration for concerned citizens. Senator Church's Committee on Intelligence Overreach chronicled the FBI's use of the media to promote propaganda during the civil rights era, and found Hoover's spying illegal. Yet more widespread and invasive surveillance is now being conducted under the premise of legality. In 2013, Edward Snowden exposed the National Security Agency's (NSA) secret surveillance on civilians, innocent or not, reportedly for national defense purposes. Subsequently, the NSA's collaboration with companies including Google, Facebook and Apple to spy on Americans was revealed to the public. Journalists have learned that the NSA has shared acquired intelligence with the FBI and other agencies to investigate crimes unrelated to national defense. In addition, some of the companies involved conduct surveillance to gather private information of citizens, which is then used to customize personalized online advertisements. What civilian information or images those companies, the NSA and law enforcement can access for other reasons is not clear. The FBI and the CIA do not elaborate on the particulars or the extent of their current use of the media.

Meanwhile, police departments across the country have been using sophisticated camera networks to monitor the public for criminal activity, which I suppose could be perceived as beneficial when used responsibly, or creepy when one considers that innocent people are also being watched.

Chapter 11
Something Like a Manhunt

A month and a half after the assassination of Dr. King, the FBI finally brought their investigation to the only country besides Mexico where a culprit fleeing by anything other than a plane or boat could have found immediate refuge. Predictably, James Earl Ray was already gone. On May 6, 1968, he had left Canada on a flight, and arrived in London the next day. After a brief excursion to Lisbon, Portugal, where he somehow managed to get the name "Sneya" changed to "Sneyd" on his passport, he returned to London. On May 27, Ray tried to rob a jewelry store, but the owners, an elderly couple, fought him off, illustrating his consistently bungling behavior.

Ray robbed a bank on June 4, but only managed to procure ninety-five pounds ($240 dollars) from the teller before running away, leaving behind his fingerprints on a paper bag.

Detective Thomas Butler led the manhunt in England. Working with various departments, he traced Ray's movements from London to Lisbon and back again. Bulletins with the fugitive's photo and aliases were sent out.

At 11:30 a.m. on June 8, James Earl Ray attempted to board a plane docked in Terminal 2 at Heathrow Airport. His destination: Brussels, Belgium, where he had been told there was an information center on mercenary operations in Africa. According to a London journalist, Ian Colvin, Ray believed that if he could get in touch with the right person,[13] then his airfare to the Congo would be paid in exchange for his mercenary service. As he presented his new passport, a British immigration officer, Kenneth Leonard Human, noticed the cancelled passport with the misspelled name in Ray's wallet. A Special Branch Officer, Phillip Birch, who was working with Human, consulted his suspect index, and then stepped in to detain the fugitive. Ray had a loaded .38 Liberty Chief Special revolver on him, but rather than engaging in a shootout or attempting to run away, he went quietly.

The Detective Chief Inspector Thompson detailed Scotland Yard's proceedings in a report to the Superintendent. During the interrogation, Detective Butler told Ray that he was wanted in connection with a murder and expressed certainty that "Sneyd" and "Galt" were aliases. Ray, who had been standing, "sat down on a bench in the cell," according to Thompson, "put his hands on his head and said, 'Oh, god.' He added after a moment or so, 'I feel so trapped.' He was again cautioned, and then said, 'Well, yes, I shouldn't say anything more now. I can't think right.' He was obviously engaged in some mental struggle, and when we left the cell, again dropped his head in his hands."

Many writers praise J. Edgar Hoover for pioneering law enforcement innovations. However, the FBI, with all of their superior technology, surveillance capabilities, ballistics division, field investigators and informants, failed to apprehend Ray in two months. It was only two *days* after the All Ports Warning in London when authorities there found him. Regarding the investigation conducted by the FBI, Judge Joe Brown would later state during *King v. Jowers* . . . "Let's put it this way: As a professional involved in the criminal justice system for a very long time, as a prosecutor, public defender, defense lawyer handling murders, robberies, very

---

[13] Ray may have been attempting to reach Major Alastair Wicks, a high-ranking officer who operated in the Belgian Congo.

serious crimes, this had to be one of the most inept and incapable, if not downright incompetent investigations, I've ever seen in my life."

After Ray's capture, civil rights proponents including Ralph Abernathy suspected a government conspiracy. In contrast, Robert Byrd, who rose to Exalted Cyclops in the anti-communist Ku Klux Klan before serving as a Senator from 1959 to 2010, asserted that the FBI had proved themselves a worthy agency and he praised them for overcoming false accusations that they had wanted King dead. "When Ray was arrested," intelligence expert William Schapp said, "then there was a state of sort of self-congratulatory columns done by the same friends of the FBI showing what a wonderful job they had done."

Segregationist George Wallace returned to the presidential race with vigor, raising over a hundred thousand dollars in front of thirteen thousand supporters in Memphis.

James Earl Ray lost his extradition hearing, which allowed the FBI to bring him back to the U.S. for a trial. The United Klans of America and the white supremacist National States Rights Party were raising funds for Ray's case, but he ended up hiring Arthur Hanes Jr., a Birmingham judge, as his lawyer.

The night before his trial, Ray fired Hanes and hired Percy Foreman. Foreman convinced Ray to plea bargain guilty to King's assassination on March 10, 1969, by asserting that a later trial in Memphis would lead to a death penalty.

Three days after Ray's conviction, which resulted in a ninety-nine year sentence, he claimed that an accomplice named Raoul pulled the trigger. A few days after that, he said that firing Arthur Hanes was the biggest mistake of his life. Ray's dozens of requests for a new trial over the next few decades were all denied.

Chapter 12
Show me the Money

An answer to the question of how James Earl Ray financed his operations would shed light on possible conspirators. The KKK had allegedly offered $100,000 to kill Dr. King, and neo-nazi groups like the Minutemen had devised similar proposals. They were never linked to Ray or the assassination.

In 1977, a man named Russell Byers claimed that the late John Sutherland had offered him $50,000 to commit the shooting, but that he had declined the offer. Sutherland was a member of the anti-civil rights John Birch Society. He had investments and holdings in Rhodesia (Zimbabwe), the heartland of apartheid, and he had been active in campaigning for segregationist George Wallace. The House Select Committee on Assassinations (HSCA) determined the claim from Byers to be "credible." Byers also said that Sutherland told him a "secret southern organization" had raised the money." However, there is no evidence that Sutherland paid James Earl Ray or even told Ray that he would pay him.

Witnesses described Ray to the FBI as homeless yet in possession of a lot of money. There are reports that he dealt drugs, although maintaining such a business as a fugitive would have been challenging and risky. He spent cash on alcohol and prostitutes, and he did successfully commit a robbery in London, but it only yielded

$240. Investigators never traced most of the $10,000 he is believed to have used in the period from his escape in 1967 to his capture in 1968.

There was a robbery in Ray's hometown, Alton, Illinois, in 1967, but police there did not consider him a suspect at the time, and he was never convicted for it. Although the HSCA determined that to be the probable source of Ray's funds. A lawyer, Gerald Posner, who has written many books that positively portray the FBI and CIA, agreed.

In 1978, the King family attorney William Pepper called East Alton police Lieutenant Walter Conrad, who said that neither Jerry Ray nor any of his brothers had ever been suspects in that robbery. Pepper later obtained an airtel from Hoover that concluded James Earl Ray's prints did not match any in the Alton bank robbery file. Yet *CNN*, the *Washington Post, Newsweek,* and the *New York Times* have all claimed or suggested, without proof, that he committed that crime.

"I think he acted alone," Hoover said early on in the investigation, "but we are not closing our minds that others might be associated with him. . . ." If Ray did take the shot without being paid for it, then the question remains, what was his motive? There are indications that he recruited voters for George Wallace and enough evidence to consider him prejudiced, but would a man with a record of committing crimes exclusively for money have chosen to take a risk that might land him in a lifetime jail sentence for no payment? It seems that the Johnson Administration, which King criticized in regard to Vietnam, and the owners of various companies that stood to lose money if economic reform were enacted, had more of a motive than Ray.

During *King v. Jowers* . . . William Pepper spoke bluntly about his conclusions: "When Martin King opposed the war, when he rallied people to oppose the war, he was threatening the bottom lines of some of the largest defense contractors in this country. This was about money. When he threatened to bring that war to a close through massive popular opposition, he was threatening the bottom lines of some of the largest construction companies, one of which was in the state of Texas, that patronized the Presidency of Lyndon Johnson and had the major construction contracts at Cam Ran Bay in Vietnam. This is what Martin King was challenging. He was challenging the weapons industry, the hardware, the armament industries, that all would lose as a result of the end of the war." A company named Brown and Root, acquired by the war contractor Halliburton in the early 1960s, funded Lyndon Johnson's career. Halliburton continued to work closely with Johnson for the duration of his presidency.

"The second aspect of his work that also dealt with money that caused a great deal of consternation in the circles of power in this land," Pepper said, "had to do with his commitment to take a massive group of people to Washington and there to encamp them in the shadow of the Washington memorial for as long as it took. For as long as it took, they would make daily trips to the halls of Congress and they would try to compel the Congress to act, as they had previously acted in terms of civil rights legislation, now to act in terms of social legislation. . . . Now, he begin to talk about a redistribution of wealth, in this the wealthiest country in the world . . ."

In 1998, as the King family were preparing for the civil case that would explore the government's involvement in the assassination, James Earl Ray died in prison, "from kidney failure and complications from liver disease," caused by Hepatitis, according to *CNN* and other major media outlets.

Chapter 13
The House Select Committee on Assassinations

Because of the hatred directed toward Martin Luther King by the FBI and prejudiced politicians, the King family suspected that members of the government had been involved in the assassination. In the continual process of trying to get to the bottom of the many inconsistencies regarding the consideration of James Earl Ray as a "lone wolf," they came to believe that Ray had not fired the fatal bullet. Among many others, William Pepper, who spent decades investigating the subject, concurred.[14]

In 1976, the House Select Committee on Assassinations (HSCA) was established to re-examine the homicides of King and the Kennedys. In 1977, the Department of Justice (DOJ) determined that the FBI's initial investigation into King's assassination was "thoroughly, honestly, and successfully conducted." Referring to who took the shot, the DOJ concluded,". . . The sum of all the evidence of Ray's guilt points to him exclusively." By 1978, the

---

[14] The suspicions of the King family may have grown following two tragedies that occurred while James Ray served his prison sentence. In July of 1969, Dr. King's brother, A.D., was found deceased in his swimming pool. Their mother passed away after being shot while playing organ during a church service in 1974.

HSCA hearings were declared complete, although numerous questionable circumstances remained unexplained.

Ed Redditt, the Memphis police officer ordered away from his surveillance of King on the day of the assassination, spoke of his testimony before the HSCA in an interview with the *Probe* journalist and activist Jim Douglass. Redditt referred to the event as a "total farce." First, he determined, based upon the questions he was asked during a closed eight-hour session, that he was testifying not to why he had been removed from the fire station, as he had assumed he was there to do, but his interrogators were focusing on discrediting him being at the fire station in the first place, even though the Memphis Police had already confirmed his presence. Following the meeting, during which Redditt expressed frustration and an unwillingness to comply with what they wanted him to say, he said that he received a phone call from a friend at the White House who told him, "Man, you're life isn't worth a wooden nickel."

The next day, when Redditt and his lawyer arrived at the hearing, they were ushered away to the executive director in charge and required to answer predetermined multiple choice questions. Said Redditt: "So in essence what they were saying was: 'This is what you're going to answer to, and this is how you're going to answer.' It was all made up—all designed, questions and answers, what to say and what not to say. A total farce."

Richard Sprague, the first chief investigator for the HSCA, was compelled to resign after saying that he would make all FBI, CIA and military agency records available. Congressman Walter Fauntroy led the sub-committee that focused on King. During the investigation, Fauntroy found electronic bugs on his television and telephone. He later said he kept his belief that Ray did not take the shot to himself because he feared for the safety of his family. At the conclusion of the HSCA hearings, Fauntroy was left with the "view that we had not explored a number of leads that were apparent to us. In the first instance, we had not been able to identify any credible witness who placed James Earl Ray at the scene . . . . We had not been able to establish that the gun which was fired at Dr. King was fired from the window above, and quite frankly, we had evidence in my judgment which was credible from three persons whose views were that the gunshot came from the bushes below. . . . Of course it was almost amusing, when we examined Mr. Ray - and I sat through hours of cross-examination of him - that Mr. Ray was really competent to be able to carry out the operation of breaking out of jail and travelling around the country and getting a hold of roughly $10,000 to sustain himself during that period and of course get - there was three passports all by himself without some help. I was disturbed also because while he could not hit a target a hundred feet away with an M-1 rifle, the marksman, or the person who shot Dr. King obviously was able to do that from about two hundred feet away so that these were questions on our minds." Ray has been repeatedly described as an inept shooter.

In an interview with Jim Douglass, Fauntroy said he reviewed his files in 1991, and found that three weeks before the assassination, J. Edgar Hoover held a series of meetings with the CIA and military intelligence.

Soon after Fauntroy spoke of his decision to write a book about what he had learned since the investigation, the Justice Department charged him with violating his financial reports while serving in Congress, based on one misdated check. He said that he thought it was a warning.

Ultimately, the HSCA concluded that Ray took the shot from the bathroom window of the rooming house across from the Lorraine Motel, that he probably had accomplices, and that "No Federal, State, or local government agency was involved in the assassination."

Chapter 14
Loyd Jowers

In 1993, former Memphis Police officer Loyd Jowers told Sam Donaldson on *Prime Time Live* that he took part in King's assassination and that Ray had been a decoy. Jowers, already retired in 1968, owned the restaurant Jim's Grill, which sat beneath the north wing of the rooming house across from the Lorraine Motel. After the *Prime Time Live* segment, SCLC staffer and politician Andrew Young, and Martin King's son, Dexter, met with a Jowers in an effort to understand the truth. They recorded the conversation for admittance during *King v. Jowers and Other Unknown Co-Conspirators*.

Jowers said that a member of the mafia, Frank Liberto, instructed him to procure the $100,000 delivered in a paper bag beneath an order of vegetables, and give it to a "Cuban" or "a wetback" the next day. The recipient was a gunrunner whom Liberto identified as "Raoul." After the produce delivery, Jowers claimed to have received a "long box" on either April 3 or 4, which he thought could have contained a rifle. He was somewhat inconsistent in explaining how he received it. At one point during the meeting, he said that Raoul brought it to him and then a few minutes later, he claimed that it arrived when he was not there.

Andrew Young believed that Jowers, who was very ill at the time of the meeting, wanted to clear his conscience before passing away. In addition, the retired officer indicated to Dexter King that he was afraid sharing the truth would land him in prison. Perhaps his contradictory account was an effort to avoid direct implication. Alternatively, maybe he simply could not recall the details precisely. In any event, he said that after keeping the long box at his restaurant for a short time, Raoul retrieved it. According to Jowers, at six p.m., April 4, he was instructed to go to the back door of his restaurant, where he heard a gunshot and then immediately received a literally smoking rifle from whom he thought was Memphis Police Officer Earl Clark.[15] Jowers said he broke the rifle down, wrapped it in a tablecloth, took the single bullet casing out, and tried to flush it down a toilet. When that did not work, he tossed the casing into the Mississippi River from atop the Mississippi Bridge. One day later, on April 5, Jowers claimed that Raoul arrived once again to recover the rifle. As far as he knew, neither the police nor the FBI ever searched his restaurant.

Regarding the type of rifle, Jowers thought it had been a 30-30 caliber but did not rule out that it could have been a 30-06, the alleged murder weapon. Inconsistencies like this have led to claims that the account from Jowers is not credible. However, despite rumors that he sought a book deal or other compensation, no evidence indicates that he received any significant payment for his statements, which, in fact, put him at legal risk.

Some of the other interesting claims Jowers made depicted additional conspirators in law enforcement. He said that secret

---

[15] To answer the question of whether or not a rifle can literally emit smoke for a period after discharge, forensic expert Judge Joe Brown said: "It is my saying that you do not get smoke from smokeless powder, but when you have a high-intensity cartridge like a 30-06, you don't, but what you might find is the following: The compression may cause a condensation of water, which is a phenomenon that I have observed from time to time hunting or shooting, or, two, you may kick up fine dust in the area immediately in front of the rifle, or, three, because the rifle slug may be moving close to the speed of sound, the shock wave from the bullet passing a bush or some foliage that has dust on it will cause it to rise and it will look to the onlooker like smoke."

meetings occurred at his restaurant, including one on the day of the assassination. The participants he implicated include the Memphis Police Homicide Chief N.E. Zachary, officers Earl Clark and Johnny Barger, an un-named stranger, men dressed in plain clothes whom he thought were FBI and CIA, and a man named Marrell McCullough (MPD officer and FBI informant).

Referring to the mafia member Frank Liberto, Jowers said, "Of course, I got to be pretty good friends with Frank, because he could do you a lot of good in Memphis, especially on the police department." Additional witnesses testified to Liberto's involvement as well.

Chapter 15
King v. Jowers and Other Unknown Co-Conspirators

Because the U.S. federal government maintains "sovereign immunity," congressional approval is required to authorize the procession of a criminal trial in which a government agency is implicated. This non-democratic doctrine, derived from an English law that states a "king can do no wrong," has been part of the American political system since the late 1700s. Scarcely has it been waived.

In 1999, the King family and their attorney William Pepper cleverly sidestepped their inability to hold the government accountable in a criminal court by opening a *civil* case against an individual. During the proceedings, the plaintiffs scrutinized the involvement of government agencies.

The complaint filed was *King Versus Jowers and Other Unknown Co-Conspirators*. Although the standards are less comprehensive in civil cases compared to criminal trials, almost seventy witnesses presented an abundance of evidence. On December 8, 1999, the jury issued the unanimous verdict that Loyd Jowers and U.S. government agencies were guilty of participating in Dr. King's assassination conspiracy.

The ruling, which would have resulted in public outrage in 1968, received scarce reaction in 1999. The repeated denial of James Earl

Ray's many trial requests had stalled legal analysis until citizens had largely forgotten the details of King's tragedy, and many of those involved were no longer alive to participate.

In addition, media coverage of *King v. Jowers and Other Unknown Co-Conspirators* was so scarce that even Americans who had not forgotten about the mysteries of King's assassination were unaware the trial had occurred. Jim Douglass, a peace activist and author of *JFK and the Unspeakable*, wrote about this case in an article first published in *Probe* magazine. He was one of only two journalists that attended the proceedings from beginning to end.

Inclusive testimony from firefighter Floyd E. Newsum scratched the surface of the dubious removal of black emergency services personnel from Fire Station no. 2 across from the Lorraine the night before and the day of King's assassination. After being inspired by King's "I've Been to the Mountaintop" speech the evening of April 3, 1968, Newsum was transferred away from Fire Station no. 2 by his lieutenant. Newsum felt confused because it left the station "out of service unless somebody else was detailed to my company in my stead." After several attempts to determine why he had been transferred, he was finally told that it was by request of the police department. When asked during the trial, "was there a police intelligence surveillance operation being conducted out of that station at the time of Martin Luther King's visit to Memphis?" He replied in the affirmative that two police officers, Richmond and Redditt, had been watching King, and "there could have been others." There was one more black firefighter stationed across from the Lorraine on April 3: Norvell E. Wallace. He too received orders to be transferred that night and testified in 1999 that he never received a reasonable explanation why. As mentioned earlier, Officer Ed Redditt, who was regularly assigned to tail and spy on Dr. King in Memphis, was also removed from his surveillance post on April 3 and April 4, 1968. Wallace testified that, like Redditt, a death threat accounted for his removal. When Wallace attempted to return to Fire Station no. 2 for clean uniforms, he said that the police had the road blocked off and would not let him pass.

Bodyguard details and tactical units were withdrawn from the area as well. Former Memphis Police Captain, Jerry Williams, testified that he was proud to have been the man in charge of the special unit of black officers that customarily provided security for King in Memphis. On April 3, 1968, Williams was told not to form his bodyguard. Years later, his Inspector told him that this "order" came after a "request" from somebody in King's entourage, who specifically asked for no black bodyguards.

Author Philip Melanson (*The Martin Luther King Assassination*) interviewed MPD Inspector Sam Evans in 1991, in an attempt to determine why the four tactical units assigned to patrol the immediate vicinity of the Lorraine Motel on April 4, 1968, were removed. Evans, now deceased, said that he gave the order at the request of Reverend Kyles, a local pastor, yet such an explanation—as well as that for the bodyguard removal—makes little sense considering that inspectors don't take orders or requests from pastors, or anyone other than their superiors, especially concerning essential matters of security. Kyles, who held no position in King's SCLC, denied making the request.

Earl Caldwell, a *New York Times* reporter that stayed at the Lorraine the night of April 4, 1968, said in videotaped testimony that he saw a man crouched and looking at the Lorraine from thick bushes across the street after the shot. He wrote an article about it, but authorities never questioned him.

Among others, former SCLC member James Orange echoed Caldwell, writing in a 1993 affidavit that after the shot, ". . . smoke came out of the brush area on the opposite side of the street from the Lorraine Motel." He "never had any doubt that the bullet was fired from the bushes." When he tried to tell police what he saw, he was told to "be quiet and get out of the way. . . ." Said Orange, "I was never interviewed or asked what I saw by any law enforcement authority in all of the time since 1968."

Solomon Jones, King's chauffer in Memphis, told the police and FBI in 1968, that soon after the shooting, he saw a man wearing a light-colored jacket hurriedly leaving the brushy area across the street from the Lorraine.

An official in the Memphis Sanitation Department, Maynard Stiles, also testified during *King v. Jowers* . . . that in the early morning of April 5, 1968, he received a call from Inspector Sam Evans who requested "assistance in clearing brush and debris" from a site he identified as the brushy area across from the Lorraine. Said Stiles, the police "proceeded with the clean up in a slow, methodical, meticulous manner."

The captain of Fire Station no. 2 in 1968, Carthel Weeden, described the two U.S. Army officers that approached him the morning of April 4. According to Weeden, the officers carried briefcases and wanted to conduct photographic work on the Lorraine. He took them to the northeast corner of the roof behind a parapet, where they had a clear view of the motel. Similarly, author and journalist Douglass Valentine declared that military intelligence veterans told him that the Army's 111th Military Intelligence Group "watched and took photos while King's assassin moved into position, took aim, fired, and walked away."

CIA operative and Iran Contra whistleblower Jack Terrell attended the trial as well. He recalled his close friend J.D. Hill confessing involvement with a sniper unit assigned to shoot "an unknown target" in Memphis on April 4. Hill was on his way to his vantage atop a water tower or one of two buildings when his unit was called back. According to Terrell, the next day, when the media broadcast widespread coverage of the assassination, Hill realized that he had been part of a backup plan to kill King if another shooter failed.

In 1979, one year after the HSCA hearings, J.D. Hill was shot to death. Law enforcement charged his wife with the crime, although she was not indicted. Terrell said that the CIA severely censored his 1992 book *Disposable Patriot*, a process that included changing a paragraph to make it look as though he believed Hill's wife had committed the shooting.

One of James Earl Ray's many attempts to appeal his case included two years of post-conviction relief hearings presided over by Judge Joe Brown in the mid 1970s. Later, in 1999, appearing under subpoena during *King v. Jowers* . . ., Brown drew from his forty years experience studying ballistics and weapons to expose some of the inconsistencies that he had found in the FBI's investigation.

Brown's ballistic tests simply did not add up. When he requested further testing, he was outraged to find that the Tennessee Court of Criminal Appeals removed him from the case under the claim that he, a black man, was biased, *not against* but *towards* James Earl Ray, who was predominantly considered to have been racist.

Regarding the bullets and cartridge cases found in the evidence bundle dropped in the entryway of Canipe's Amusement Company compared to the bullet found in Dr. King's body, he said, ". . . there were four unfired cartridge cases that were recovered along with the rifle and one fired cartridge case. A primitive metallurgical test done some thirty years ago revealed or suggests that the fired *cartridge case* and the four unfired *cartridge cases* are metallurgically identical, that is, they are from the same lot. The *bullets* from the four unfired cartridge cases are metallurgically identical when the lead cores are analyzed, whereas the *bullet* removed from Dr. King is not identical [emphasis added]. It is metallurgically different in its composition, which would suggest it is not from the same lot . . . That suggests that this bullet was not fired from that empty cartridge case that was found with the rifle . . ."

Furthermore, Brown said, "There was a picture of the bullet or the slug that was removed from Dr. King's body before it was transmitted to the FBI. That picture revealed that the bullet was intact, though mushroomed. What the FBI sent back at the conclusion of the test was three jacket fragments and three lead core fragments that had been cut as though you were taking a banana and just peeled the peels all the way off of the banana and then took a knife and cut the banana lengthwise in three equal sections."

In reference to the rifle James Earl Ray allegedly used for the assassination, Brown said, "Now, there was also an FBI report in the record that talked about this weapon having been test fired shortly after it was taken into evidence. And that report revealed that it shot several feet to one side at a hundred yards and slightly half that low. So this does not appear to have been a sighted-in weapon." This meant that the rifle could not have accurately fired a bullet. "It is my opinion," Brown said, "that this is not the murder weapon."

Those interested in exploring the statements of numerous additional witnesses may refer to the complete transcript of *King v. Jowers and Other Unknown Co-Conspirators*.

Chapter 16
Raoul

In a 1995 deposition, James Earl Ray spoke in detail about the man he claimed set him up and committed the assassination. Ray said that "Raoul" gave him money for a white Mustang and a rifle during the summer of 1967, in Montreal, and guided his stalking of King.

Loyd Jowers identified Raoul in a scattering of photographs as the man who had brought him the rifle at Jim's Grill. Additional witnesses also said that the man in the same photo was a gunrunner they knew as Raoul.

Author Philip Melanson has suggested that "Raoul" might have been an alias for Jules "Ricco" Kimble, who admitted to knowing Ray and participating in the conspiracy. Kimble never came out on his own, but spoke of his role only after documentarians John Sergeant and John Edginton tracked him down for an interview, which indicates that his statements were not financially motivated.

Kimble disclosed that he worked for the CIA as a pilot, courier, and assassin.[16] He said that Ray was a set up man whom he had

---

[16] Kimble claimed to have committed two political assassinations for the CIA in Canada. The HSCA found that the FBI, the CIA, and the Royal Canadian Mounted Police all had a file on Kimble.

flown from Atlanta to Montreal in July of 1967. There, said Kimble, a CIA specialist provided Ray with numerous aliases. However, when Sergeant and Edginton provided a photograph and asked Ray about Kimble's claim, Ray looked away, then glanced at the picture nervously before saying, "No, there's no truth in that whatsoever. I don't know, I've never had any contact with him. I've possibly . . . I've seen him but I don't even recall that, and there is . . . He may be in some type of . . . Is he in prison now? . . . Well, there's a possibility that he's under some pressure from the government. He may know something about the King case, but he's trying to disinformation [sic] things of that nature."

Unfortunately, Ray's characteristically meandering response failed to shed clarity on the issue. His behavior depicted anxiety, yet recognition as well as confusion. Was he simply reluctant to snitch on an accomplice? Did he believe that he would be further implicated if he admitted to knowing Kimble, or that he would be killed if he spoke of certain people or circumstances? Was Kimble lying to Sergeant and Edginton, or attempting to create misdirection? Whether or not adequate answers to these questions exist, Kimble does offer one possible explanation for how Ray obtained various fraudulent identities and passports. The opposing theory that Ray acted alone is plausible only if one can accept that a fugitive may have the time and means to commit complicated crimes by himself on the run, without being caught for two months. Ray's unknown source of money and bungling history are additional factors to consider.

At the end of *King v. Jowers* . . . , William Pepper said in his closing statement, "Now, as I understand it, the defense has invited Raoul to appear here. He is outside this jurisdiction, so a subpoena would be futile. But he was asked to appear here. In earlier proceedings there were attempts to depose him, and he resisted them. So he has not attempted to come forward at all and tell his side of the story or to defend himself."

Chapter 17
The Many Faces of a Photograph

According to numerous sources, immediately after King's assassination, a man nearby named Joseph Louw took a series of photographs. One such photo depicts three men standing beside a fallen King. They are pointing towards the sound of the gunshot they had just heard, upward, seemingly higher and further to the right than the bathroom of the rooming house where authorities say James Ray fired the bullet. This particular direction can be determined by comparing the location of the men beside King with the angle of their arms and photographs of the local environment. Curiously, the men are also not pointing to the brushy area, where witnesses claimed to have seen evidence of an assassin.

Two of the three men with raised arms in the photo are SCLC members Andrew Young and Ralph Abernathy. Another man in that picture, who is kneeling, checking King's pulse, has been identified as Darrell McCullough by SCLC member James Orange, among others. McCullough, whose name is spelled differently in various sources, was known as an undercover Memphis Police officer in 1968, during which time he served as an FBI informant. He is alleged to have infiltrated the Invaders and instigated the violence during the Memphis riot. He also worked for the CIA, beginning, at least, in 1974.[17]

The photograph, incidentally, was published in *Time*, one of the media outlets that Pulitzer Prize winning journalist Carl Bernstein said the CIA used for propaganda. In addition, a photographer named Ernest Withers, who chronicled Dr. King's activities, was later exposed as an FBI informant. According to an article by Nick Allen in *The Telegraph*, Joseph Louw, "who took a picture on the balcony moments after the shooting, went to Withers who developed the image in his dark room." Such an association casts doubt on the credibility of the frequently circulated image, considering that the FBI and CIA used the media to facilitate propaganda.

---

[17] SCLC member James Orange wrote in a 1993 affidavit: "James Bevel and I were driven around by Marrell McCullough, a person who at the time we knew to be a member of The Invaders, a local community organizing group, and who we subsequently learned was an undercover agent for the Memphis Police Department and who now works for the Central Intelligence Agency."

Orange: "From that day [of the assassination, April 4th, 1968] to this time [1993] I have never had any doubt that the fatal shot, the bullet which ended Dr. King's life, was fired by a sniper concealed in the brush area behind the derelict buildings. I also remember then turning my attention back to the balcony and seeing Marrell McCullough up on the balcony kneeling over Dr. King looking as though he was checking Dr. King for life signs."

A section regarding the findings on the MLK assassination in the National Archives states: "Marrell McCullough, the undercover Memphis police officer whose intelligence on the Invaders was transmitted regularly to the local FBI office, was in the parking lot of the Lorraine Motel at the time of the assassination and was among the first to reach the fallen Dr. King."

Lisa Pease, co-author of *The Assassinations* has chronicled a PrimeTime segment in which Sam Donaldson called the CIA and asked for McCullough, who came to the phone. During the conversation, McCullough confirmed that he knew Loyd Jowers. When Donaldson mentioned that his inquiry pertained to King, McCullough ceased to communicate.

Chapter 18
Who Did It?

The FBI and Memphis police committed malicious acts that specifically targeted black citizens. In addition, their investigations as well as those of the House Select Committee on Assassinations, are riddled with inconsistencies and missing information. Yet such authorities are often perceived or depicted as credible. Therefore, their conclusion that James Earl Ray fired the fatal bullet from the bathroom window of the rooming house is commonly reported as truth among the media. However, as previously illustrated, numerous eyewitnesses claimed that the shot came from the brushy area.

Could it be that authorities planted decoys in the bushes to support evidence that the shot was not taken from the rooming house window, in order to help draw attention away from an assassin that fired from a third, more distant location? Such a counterintelligence tactic, while speculation, remains in the realm of possibility. One may also theorize that a loud "blank" was fired from a location upward and to the right of the rooming house to take attention away from a bullet fired simultaneously from the bushes. However, a definitive answer regarding the source of the shot has not been determined.

Some writers have suggested that the sound of the gunshot reverberated off local structures, making the source indecipherable.

There were no structures in the space between where James Earl Ray supposedly lurked, and where King stood on the balcony of the Lorraine across the street.

An engineering survey on the path of the bullet provided inconclusive results. Engineers did determine, however, that "the probable posture of Dr. King at the instant of impact" was "head forward looking down into the parking area and with a slight forward bend at the waist."

The King family and their attorney William Pepper believed that Ray did not take the shot and that the FBI, local police, and Army Intelligence were involved. Nobody has explored this subject as extensively as the King family, whose reputations of integrity are well established. In addition, the verdict from *King v. Jowers and Other Unknown Co-Conspirators* supported their stance.

Martin King's son, Dexter, agreed with the indication of Loyd Jowers that the Memphis Police officer, Earl Clark, was the shooter, while "members of a Special Forces team . . . didn't have to act because the contract killer succeeded."

James Ray's history clearly shows that he committed crimes exclusively for money. Therefore, whether he or a contract killer pulled the trigger, whoever did it was, in all likelihood, paid well for the job. The most relevant question then becomes, who paid the assassin? That has not been answered. Numerous people in a chain of payment could have allowed a kingpin benefactor to remain nearly impossible to trace, particularly if some of those people operated under aliases. Of course, there are other means by which money can be made untraceable and criminals can muddle their tracks.

Ultimately, however, several people and circumstances contributed to Dr. King's tragic passing. J. Edgar Hoover knowingly consented to engage in criminal activity including illegal wiretapping and microphone surveillance. He was likely involved in the malicious letter intended to convince Dr. King to commit suicide, which repeatedly stated "you are done." Additionally, although King never committed any federal crimes, Hoover's FBI persistently slandered and hounded the civil rights leader.[18] What lengths would Hoover have been willing to entertain? To what level can he be considered guilty?

Regardless of how one chooses to answer those questions, the attitude of the most powerful law enforcement figure in the country trickled down through the ranks in accordance with procedure. When the author of the "suicide letter," Agent William Sullivan, testified during Senator Church's Committee on Intelligence Overreach in the mid 1970s as to whether anyone in the FBI opposed Hoover's tactics, he replied, "Everybody in the division went right along with Hoover's policy. . . . never once did I hear anybody, including myself, raise the question, is this course of action which we have agreed upon lawful, is it legal, is it ethical or moral? . . . I think this suggests really in government we are amoral."

Like FBI agents acting under orders, and probably many police officers, a large portion of American people simply believed reports that depicted King as an insurgent without looking into the matter personally. Therefore, it should be recognized that the common inclination to accept a belief simply because the source is the news or an authority figure, rather than because supportive facts exist, has allowed J. Edgar Hoover, and even historical figures including Adolf Hitler, to effectively foster hateful causes. Law enforcement personnel, as well as most workers and students, are trained to follow orders, not question them, which indicates that such citizens are more likely to follow a malicious order compared to those inclined to question authority. Such behavior speaks of the risks compliance encompasses.[19]

---

[18] In addition to a number of arrests during peaceful demonstrations, King received a jail sentence in the *state* of Alabama for parading without a permit.

[19] In 1960, Dr. Stanley Milgram conducted experiments in which 65% of subjects complied with the orders of an authority to inflict what they understood to be an extreme administration of electric shock (450 volts) upon hypothetical personnel in a different room. Although nobody suffered harm, the subjects believed the opposite and predominantly followed orders. Furthermore, all of the participants administered twenty shocks, agreeing to 300 volts. In subsequent experiments, Milgram placed the subjects in the same room as an actor playing the part of

Memphis Mayor, Henry Loeb, Police Director, Frank Holloman, and many of the Memphis police repeatedly participated in or enabled violence against black civilians. At the very least, these authorities enhanced racial conflict by setting the example that the needs of non-whites, including most of the striking sanitation workers, were irrelevant.

The exact involvement of the CIA and Army Intelligence is difficult to trace despite their links to the crime.

Loyd Jowers, who admitted to being part of the assassination conspiracy, is guilty, although his willingness to speak out and atone for his actions when so many others have remained silent is commendable. Of course, James Earl Ray is guilty as well. Even if he did not pull the trigger, he was involved. Ironically, however, Ray was raised in an impoverished and uneducated family that characterized the social maladies King wanted to solve.[20]

Dr. King had traced aspects of poverty and inequality to American economic and foreign policy, and that may have been his most formidable opponent. Lyndon Johnson's relationship with Halliburton and his commitment to Vietnam in order to "avoid humiliating U.S. defeat"— as Assistant Defense Secretary John McNaughton wrote in the Pentagon Papers—not only took government funds away from many possible political reformations, but it literally killed thousands of soldiers and innocent civilians.[21]

---

victim and forty percent inflicted the maximum damage. In addition to illustrating how dangerous compliance can be, Milgram concluded it was not just Nazis that had the capacity to commit atrocious acts simply by following orders, but Americans as well.

[20] The Ray family reportedly burned the framework of their home for heat during a severe winter.

[21] Daniel Ellsberg, a former analyst for the Pentagon, leaked a plethora of previously confidential information in 1971. Among the disclosure known as the Pentagon Papers, Assistant Defense Secretary John McNaughton wrote that the U.S. intentions in Vietnam were "70% - - to avoid humiliating U.S. defeat. 20% - - to keep SVN (South Vietnam) territory from Chinese hands. 10% - - to permit the people of SVN to enjoy a better, freer way of life. Also - - to emerge from crisis without unacceptable taint from methods used." Although McNaughton did not

William Pepper made a strong case that King's opposition to the Johnson administration was an instrumental factor in the assassination.

Defense contracting continues to be a lucrative business. The companies that currently work with the American government in such a capacity—Lockheed Martin, Boeing, General Dynamics, among others—have a financial incentive to engage in war. Although infrastructure and industrial products are required in wartime, those who invest in, and work for these companies do also profit from foreign conflicts. This condition provides such beneficiaries a reason to condone the political possibility of lingering longer than necessary in war. (The first word that appears as an autocomplete suggestion after typing "Lockheed Martin" into a Google search is "jobs," the second is "stock.") [22] Unfortunately, despite those that donate portions of profits to charity, companies providing financial incentives to employees interested in promoting tolerance, non-violence, and equal rights, are hard to find.

Dexter King made a significant point when he said, " . . . it is not about who killed Martin Luther King Jr., my father. It is not necessarily about all of those details. It is about: *Why* was he killed? Because if you answer the why, you will understand the same things are still happening. Until we address that, we're all in trouble. Because if it could happen to him . . . if it can happen to this family, it can happen to anybody."

The why indicates that there is often more beneath the surface of a story. Understanding the why fosters the recognition that our government and the financial elite utilize media propaganda to convince citizens of things that are not true. The why tells us that politics and business is competitive, complicated, and sometimes

---

mention financial interests in this written record, the strategy he indicated revealed that, contrary to what President Johnson told the public, promoting the benevolent ideals of democracy did not account for the motivation behind America's continued presence in Vietnam.

[22] Regional popular searches formulate autocomplete suggestions. Eugene, Oregon served as the location of the author's search.

ruthless. And the why exposes the abominable human capacity to neglect the sanctity of life, a behavior that can be taught to any child. Perhaps, pinning a horrible tragedy on one drunk, racist man takes attention away from the why and nurtures a communal desire for simple explanations.

Chapter 19
The "Big" Picture

As Dr. King demonstrated, equality, or a lack thereof, is connected to economics. Financial equality implies that workers deserve a larger slice of the pie than the owners of companies predominantly want to pay. Subsequently, equity threatens the profits of the financial elite and the careers of politicians funded by corporate donors.

Slavery contributed to the initial development of the United States. Before the civil war, cotton accounted for more than half of all the profits from American exports. By 1840, the United States provided 60 percent of the world's cotton. In the more progressive north, textile factories, meat processors, the insurance industry, exporters, and brokers all prospered from slavery.

When abolition made free labor obsolete, owners were compelled to utilize the cheapest possible labor to maximize profits. That practice has not changed.

The Civil Rights Era stimulated the most recent possibility of significant economic reform. Unfortunately, the assassination of Martin Luther King in 1968 foreshadowed an increasingly concerning financial situation for a broad majority of citizens. Since then, Americans have worked progressively more hours and more family members have had to become employed. Despite claims that the problems of the lower class are rooted in laziness, from 1973 to 2014, workers' net productivity grew 72.2 percent, according to the Economic Policy Institute. From 1979 to 2013, inflation skyrocketed 203 percent, wages for the top earning 1 percent increased 138 percent while the bottom 90 percent saw only a 15 percent rise.[23] Corporate profits as a percentage of American and worldwide income have continually escalated as well. A 2015 Credit Suisse report concluded that the richest 1 percent owned half the world's wealth. More recently, an OXFAM paper illustrated, "82 percent of all of the growth in global wealth in the last year [2017] went to the top 1 percent, whereas the bottom 50 percent saw no increase at all."

Corporate taxes have been high, officially, for a long time in America. For example, in 1937, near the end of the depression, the federal tax rate for corporations that earned over $40,000 annually was 15 percent. By 1949, corporate tax rates had risen to 38 percent for those that earned over $50,000. In 2017, corporations that earned over $18,333,333 were taxed 35 percent by the federal government. Including state taxes, that number increased to 39.2 percent. In the same year, *individuals* that earned more than $418,400 were also taxed 39 percent. Large corporations benefit from high-tech automation, as well as economies of scale and scope. They also save money paying low wages, in some cases to children. Individuals do not often have such advantages.

In addition, "Thanks to things like tax credits, exemptions and offshore tax havens," CNN's James O'Toole wrote, "the actual tax burden of American companies is much lower." The Government Accountability Office (GAO) found, in 2010, profitable American corporations paid only an average of 12.6 percent in domestic federal taxes. War contractors Boeing and General Electric, as well as the

---

[23] The economic gap these statistics indicate is more drastic when one considers that the top 1 percent derive much of their wealth from sources other than wages, including ownership, investments, and tax havens.

communications company Verizon, paid zero federal income tax from 2008 to 2012. [24]

Two hundred fifty-eight of the Fortune 500 corporations were consistently profitable between 2008 and 2015. The Institute on Taxation and Economic Policy (ITEP) reported, "the 258 corporations paid an [average] effective federal income tax rate of 21.2 percent over the eight-year period." That is about 60 percent of the official statutory rate. The report also determined: "Eighteen of the corporations, including General Electric, International Paper, Priceline.com and PG&E, paid no federal income tax at all over the eight-year period. A fifth of the corporations (48) paid an effective tax rate of less than 10 percent over that period." In 2015, twenty-nine corporations paid no income tax. Among those were Netflix, PG&E, and Exxon Mobil.

The new tax plan, backed by Trump, offers a 21 percent federal rate for corporations, which turns out to be almost exactly what was effectively paid previously. However, it seems unlikely that the leaders of corporations will suddenly decide profits are no longer important and discontinue utilizing tax credits, exemptions and tax havens. Therefore, it may follow that corporations will continue to pay sixty percent of the statutory tax rate. That would lower the rate corporations actually pay now to 12.6 percent. Even if circumstances increase what corporations pay to 80 percent the statutory rate, the result would be 16.8 percent, which is five percent less than what an individual that makes between 38,700 and 82,500 pays as of 2018.

Ultimately, the less taxes corporations pay, the more individuals with far less money will be responsible for making up the difference in federal funds.

---

[24] From 2008 to 2012, Boeing, General Electric and Verizon were consistently among the fifteen highest spending lobbyists.

Chapter 20
The Wormtongue Fellowship

Nobody in America has exerted the same level of influence in promoting equity since Dr. King. That void has allowed some of the same forces who opposed him to continually mislead the public. One of those is the John Birch Society (JBS), a traditionally anti-civil rights organization currently dedicated to preventing the dangers of "big government."

When the *Brown v. Board of Education* decision (1954) resulted in the desegregation of schools, the John Birch Society called for the supreme court justice to be impeached. The movement to enact civil rights during the 1960s, according to the JBS, was a communist plot to promote ". . . the Negro Soviet Republic" in cities including Memphis. They claimed that our Federal Government was "already, literally, in the hands of communists," including President Eisenhower. After a compelling 2009 movie about a South African rugby team, the JBS posted an article on their website that called Nelson Mandela, "nothing more than a communist terrorist thug . . ."

One of the high-ranking and instrumental members of the JBS was Fred Koch, who, in 1958, participated in developing a more efficient method for the thermal cracking of crude oil. He previously took part in building an oil refinery for the Nazi regime of Adolf Hitler. A year after he passed away, his company was renamed Koch

Industries. Today, Koch Industries is controlled by two of his sons, Charles and David, who have amassed a combined net worth of $120 billion building oil pipelines, and investing in real estate, chemicals, cattle, and coal mining, among other industries. In 2005, Koch Industries bought the synthetic materials and paper products giant, Georgia Pacific, for $21 billion.[25]

It was not simply the buying and selling of goods in a "free market" that prompted the rise of the Koch brothers to the top of the billionaire list. The prosperity they were born into has been bolstered by an immense "information" campaign to promote their financial interests through a wide array of websites, foundations, think tanks, universities, and scientific institutions. Some of the most prominent organizations the Kochs and their allies have utilized include the Tea Party, Americans for Prosperity (AFP),[26] the American Enterprise Institute, the Heartland Institute, the Heritage Foundation, the U.S. Chamber of Commerce, the Institute for Justice, the Institute for Humane Studies, the Bill of Rights Institute, the Cato Institute, the Competitive Enterprise Institute, the Center to Protect Patient Rights, the American Petroleum Institute, and the Independent Women's Forum.

The Koch brothers have been outspoken in their desire to maintain the American "free market." A statement on the home page of the Koch Industries website indicates, "We challenge ourselves to improve people's lives by creating better products using fewer resources. At the same time, we challenge barriers that hinder competition, opportunity, innovation and progress."

Closer inspection reveals a more accurate agenda. Specifically, the Koch brothers spend a lot of money and energy fostering opposition to particular political issues. They are against chemical regulations, cap and trade legislation to reduce pollution and

---

[25] Georgia Pacific has the distinction of being one of the top producers of the known carcinogen formaldehyde.

[26] Journalist Lee Fang investigated the modern Tea Party and found that it had originated in Americans for Prosperity, an organization that portrayed itself as "grassroots" despite big business donors.

emissions, limits on corporate spending to influence politics, higher taxes on the most wealthy, labor unions, health care reform, and programs for the impoverished. According to their perspectives, and those with similar financial interests, any government that attempts to implement such humanitarian regulation or reform is "too big" and suspiciously close to a communist state, or possibly a dictatorship.

The U.S. Constitution indicates that one of the responsibilities of congress is to "regulate commerce with foreign nations, and among the several states, and with the Indian tribes." Current regulations can be tedious, occasionally unnecessary, and aggravating to business owners. Furthermore, there are conditions in America that point to totalitarian threats of federal executive power. One is "sovereign immunity," which allows our government to deny the procession of a criminal trial in which it is implicated.

Eminent domain gives the government authority to take control of private property for public and procedural purposes. The federal government, in 2015, owned 28% of all land in the United States.

The National Security Agency (NSA) continues to collaborate with communications companies to conduct surveillance on civilians, innocent or otherwise. The resultant information is not only shared with various law enforcement and government agencies, but it is also used by the companies involved for advertising purposes.

Additionally, until 2014, it was FBI policy to refrain from audio recording or videotaping interrogation interviews, which would alternatively be summarized by agents in what were termed FD-302 documents. Now, four exceptions that exempt the FBI from being legally compelled to provide electronic evidence remain. Other agencies, including the CIA, are also not required to supply electronic proof of interrogations. This procedure has prevented lawyers, journalists and students from accessing facts about the Martin Luther King assassination and other important events.[27] It

---

[27] Many police departments across the country have enacted progressive recording practices, although they are not always enforced. For example, after a policy that required recording suspect interviews was implemented in Iowa, a survey found that police had complied only about half of the time. To cite another example,

also takes away one method by which a wrongfully accused citizen can obtain advantageous evidence.

When the Koch-funded foundations speak of the necessity for a "limited government," they mention little of these issues, rather, they focus on portraying any oversight of the products they sell as a threat to the free market.

Analyzing the Koch rhetoric and tracing the money they spend lobbying reveals three notable points. First, they stimulate fear of "big-government" communism or socialism in order to sway voters to their industry-friendly perspective, echoing anti-civil rights efforts by the FBI, which convinced a number of Americans that Dr. King was a dangerous communist.[28] Second, the interests the Kochs promote correlate exactly with supporting the products they sell, rather than preserving American freedom. Third, their ideals are aligned with those of the John Birch Society.

The Koch-controlled Americans for Prosperity tag line is, "We protect the American Dream by fighting each day for lower taxes, less government regulation and economic prosperity for all." It is not mentioned specifically that they are fighting regulations on carcinogenic chemicals and pollutants that contribute to climate change.

The Cato Institute describes itself as a think tank "dedicated to the principles of individual liberty, limited government, and peace." The Heritage Foundation is another Koch "think tank," whose mission is

---

New York City created a procedure in 2012 to videotape interviews of murder, sex crime, and felony suspects. However, an article in the *New York Times* revealed that one year afterwards, only twenty-eight of seventy-six detective squads in the city had recording equipment set up in their interview rooms.

[28] While both communism and socialism advocate equality in theory, in a communist state, the government owns production, land and transportation. The online Oxford Dictionary additionally states that communism is "A political theory derived from Karl Marx, advocating class war . . ." While Marx participated in developing communism, the theory does not advocate class war. Socialism is more of an economic concept applicable to various political systems. It allows individuals to buy and sell private property and possessions, and to have influence in the proceedings of public property, including factories.

to "advance the principles of free enterprise, limited government, individual freedom, traditional American values, and a strong national defense."

Similarly, the John Birch Society intends "To bring about less government, more responsibility, and—with God's help—a better world by providing leadership, education, and organized volunteer action in accordance with moral and constitutional principles."

It is often considered inappropriate to assume that children adopt the ideals of their parents. Although Fred Koch was part of the prejudiced JBS, and built infrastructure for Nazis, that does not necessarily mean that Charles and David Koch are also prejudiced. However, the unprecedented amount they spent opposing America's first black president made a lot of people wonder whether they do embrace discrimination, or if they simply oppose progressive ideals to secure profits. According to the Center for Public Integrity, Americans for Prosperity spent $122 million to foil the efforts of Barack Obama and political democrats in 2012. In its previous eight years AFP spent only $72 million overall.

Some argue that the use of the media and the ability to influence politics are powers deservedly earned in a free market. Although the question remains whether those involved in criminal activity deserve such power.

Koch-controlled companies have been convicted of fraud and price fixing, in addition to malice and negligence in a case that involved a faulty butane pipeline which caused the deaths of two Texas teenagers. The company has paid numerous fines relating to environmental destruction, and even used a foreign subsidiary and their status as a private company to conduct business with Iran, which is categorized as a "terrorist state" by the U.S. Department of State.[29] [30]

---

[29] Various sources, including articles in the *New Yorker* by Jane Mayer, and an enlightening expose in *Bloomberg Markets*, elaborated on the nefarious activities conducted by the Koch brothers. In addition to those already mentioned, Koch Industries paid a thirty million dollar civil fine to settle accusations that they discharged three million gallons of oil into American waterways in the mid 1990s. The Kochs plea-bargained to pay a twenty million dollar fine in connection with a

Since Charles and David Koch are prominent lobbyists, their industry-friendly policies find sympathizers in government. Because of their subsequent market power, their transgressions and influence reach every corner of America, impacting taxes and consumer prices, enabling pollution, compromising the health and health care of citizens. In contrast, a black man dressed in urban attire who, for example, illegally sells cigarettes, harms only those in his neighborhood who choose to buy his products. He is also a mere microcosm of the companies that legally sell far more of the same harmful products.[31]

Department of Justice indictment that they had covered up the release of ninety-one tons of the carcinogenic benzene from a refinery in Texas. They have paid bribes to receive contracts. David Koch has donated to various cancer charities and, until 2010, sat on the National Cancer Institute advisory board while simultaneously lobbying for lax chemical regulations, particularly to prevent the categorization of formaldehyde as a known carcinogen, which the EPA determined it to be in 2011.

The Koch brothers have exerted financial influence to promote their particular interests in various educational institutions, including George Mason's Mercatus Center, a non-profit that advertises itself as "bridging the gap between academic ideas and real-world problems."

David Koch's donated money to the Smithsonian's National Museum of National History led to a prominent environmental display that depicted a human history of adapting to natural climate changes without mentioning anything about manmade causes of climate change, or his financial interests in such causes.

Because Koch Industries is a private company—second most profitable to Cargill in America—they are not required to reveal their financial information. Most of what we know about them has been revealed by independent organizations and persistent journalists, however, the full extent of their operations and influence is unknown.

[30] After the superb journalist, Jane Mayer, published incriminating work on the Koch Brothers, their associates attempted to slander her as a plagiarist. The plan backfired when the journalists whose words Mayer allegedly stole revealed the charges false.

[31] In 2014, NYPD Officer Daniel Panteleo caused the death of Eric Garner by placing a chokehold on him and then failing to relent after the restrained man gasped eleven times, "I can't breathe." Other officers contributed by constricting the victim's chest.

Many Americans have recognized the non-democratic reality that lobbying and media control provide the financial elite with extreme political influence. Yet it does not seem to matter whether the majority of people see wealth in politics as negative. In 2010, industry interests won *Citizens United v. Federal Election Commission* (FEC), cleverly portraying themselves as ordinary "citizens" fighting a "big government" villain, the FEC. The verdict enabled unlimited spending to use the media for the purpose of swaying voters, offering a greater advantage to the most wealthy, and allowing entities including the Koch brothers to continually conduct their massive "information" campaign. As the significance of this ruling has reached the public, it is evident that citizens are not united with industry on the matter. A 2015 national poll conducted by Bloomberg Politics found that 78% of Americans wanted Citizens United overturned. Democratic and Republican respondents predominantly agreed on the issue.

Garner, who had a history of selling cigarettes illegally, had been attempting to understand what evidence warranted his harassment that particular day and expressed verbal frustration accentuated by arm gestures when the officers did not have an adequate answer. Although the media frequently reported, with various action verbs, that Garner resisted arrest, full versions of the video of the event, which are publicly available, clearly show that when backup arrived and the officers decided to physically engage, Garner said, "Don't touch me please. Do not touch me," while moving his hands in a gently evasive manner, and then ceasing to move after he was momentarily restrained and wrestled to the sidewalk, where the choke hold remained in place long enough to inflict fatal damage.

In the fiscal year 2015 to 2016, taxes on cigarettes generated an estimated $1.2 billion in New York.

Chapter 21
Commuphobia

Industry spokespeople have argued that government agencies including the FEC exert too much control over free enterprise and that excessive regulations foreshadow communism. In contrast, proponents of the general welfare refer to economic statistics to show that it is immense companies—like Koch Industries, Cargill, Walmart, Exxon Mobil, Pfizer, and JPMorgan Chase—that have too much power over our government and the market, consequently creating an economic dictatorship in which the financial elite continue to prosper at the expense of the vast majority of people.

In the early 1940s, equal rights proponent Henry A. Wallace gained considerable recognition for his progressive views while serving as vice president. His opponents, including President Truman, later defamed him as a communist sympathizer. Now, few people are aware he existed, not to mention that he was a brilliant man who played an instrumental role in digging America out of the Great Depression and contributed to breakthroughs in science, farming and nutrition.[32] Eisenhower, John Kennedy, Martin Luther King, and Barack Obama all suffered the same communist accusations. Yet none of them, nor Wallace, ever displayed credible evidence of attempting to turn America into a communist state.[33]

At the end of World War II, and for a short period thereafter, the United States maintained a monopoly on the atomic bomb. When Russia inevitably acquired the same nuclear technology, the American government faced a dilemma. The same colossal destruction that had been authorized in Washington against Hiroshima and Nagasaki could now be as recklessly unleashed at home. Although Russia had been an ally during the war, the Truman Doctrine, among other actions, made it clear that the United States was subsequently disinterested in continuing to collaborate with the communist country, which had lost far more people than America in its relentless struggle against the nazis. The nazis no longer presented a problem, however, they had been neutralized. It was the communists that President Truman, Director of the Manhattan Project Leslie Groves, J. Edgar Hoover, and other members of the government now feared as the primary threat to capitalism and the republic. When China adopted communism in 1949, this fear, coupled with an aggressive American nationalism, grew—along with the Cold War—and lingered in the minds of authorities including Hoover, who had already been serving the House Un-American Activities Committee in an effort to abolish the small communist movement in the United States.[34]

When the civil rights crusade commenced in 1955, Hoover's fixation had not diminished. Like a Russian, Dr. King came from a

---

[32] In addition to his service as vice president from 1941 to 1945 during the presidency of Franklin D. Roosevelt, Henry A. Wallace held the offices of secretary of agriculture (1933-1940), and secretary of commerce (1945-1946).

[33] It should be noted that speaking with a communist, or recognizing wealth inequality, does not make one a communist.

[34] In 1942, the Communist Party of the United States of America reached its height of 85,000 members, only 0.063% of 134.9 million citizens.

different ethnic background compared to most American authorities of white Western European ancestry. King's philosophy indicated that impoverished citizens deserved the equal opportunity to earn the same privileges as the elite. He spoke eloquently to expose social injustice, criticized authorities that abused their power, and embodied the courage to conduct civil disobedience. Perhaps such factors made it appear to Hoover that the civil rights leader was working with communists to infiltrate the country from within, rather than simply attempting to enact humanitarian reform. Or maybe Hoover privately knew that King was not a communist but indignity, prejudice, and paranoia motivated the accusation. Nevertheless, King did assert that the solutions for exploitation did not include communism.

In addition, there may have been economic concerns behind the FBI's slanderous media campaign. William Pepper wrote about politically influential entities including Halliburton, the banking industry and oil tycoons, H.L. Hunt and Clint Murchison, all of whom profited from the Vietnam War, which King wanted to end. President Johnson, whose commitment to the war King criticized, was not only funded by Halliburton. Hunt and Murchison were also among his major benefactors, and friends with Johnson's one time neighbor, J. Edgar Hoover.

Today, the Koch brothers and other financial leaders—in chemicals, banking, pharmaceuticals, agribusiness, and oil—establish a public fear of communism to avoid "big government" regulation on products and economic policies profitable to themselves, yet often detrimental to the majority of citizens. This strategy, more evident in the modern landscape, depends on the media to garner voter support. Such voter support inhibits regulations on fossil fuels, chemicals, commercialized animal agriculture, oil drilling, and deforestation, all of which are profitable to Koch Industries, among others, and man-made causes of climate change according to overwhelming scientific consensus.[35]

---

[35] Although industries attempt to profit from any new trend, including environmentalism, the Koch brothers and ExxonMobil are among the most prominent financial forces in the country, and their wealth has been tremendously

Commuphobia can also compromise Dr. King's dream of a reasonable minimum wage and adequate health care.

Now that dedicated journalists like Jane Meyer and Lee Fang have exposed the Koch strategy, a new means to promote the corporate perspective has emerged: Donald Trump. Seemingly unaware that regulatory agencies provide jobs, the president has been blatantly dismantling what he calls "job-destroying" regulations. Despite claims that Trump is not allied with the Koch brothers and similar interests, his environmental cutbacks, appointments, and tax plan indicate that he is.[36]

---

augmented as a result of lack of regulation on manmade causes of climate change. Claims that Al Gore, James Cameron and green energy companies have created fear of climate change for profit stand futile in contrast.

[36] The Koch-funded Heritage Foundation proudly proclaims on their website that they influenced policies adopted by theTrump Administration.

Chapter 22
A Proper Phrase

Because most citizens do not have the wealth required to exert significant political influence, America cannot be reasonably referred to as a democracy. In addition, it is debatable whether a free market exists any place only a portion of the population is born with the ability to invest.

If imminent legislation to eliminate all private property existed, and the government nearly owned all national production and transportation, then it would be accurate to consider America close to a communist state. The federal government actually owned 3.9% less land in 2015 compared to 1990. Communism, in theory, indicates that goods and wealth are controlled by the government and equally distributed among the people. Subsequently, the implementation of communism would require congress to authorize less money for themselves, which is unlikely.

Ironically, by paying congress and financing campaigns, big-industry owns the government, not the opposite. Yet the government has the power to enact industry-friendly legislation. Therefore, it is not the government *or* corporate powers that compromise democracy, but both are willing partners in a marriage of interests.

Despite the fact that influential corporate entities, which comprise a small percentage of society, use extreme power and the media to sway voters and lawmakers, citizens still have the ability to vote, whether for their own interests or those of a persuasive group. Therefore, the proper phrase for our current political system is an oligarchic republic. Admittedly, that does not exactly roll off the tongue.

Chapter 23
Renewing the Dream

Financial hardship and racial dissent interfere with the ability of Americans to unify and foster reform. A reinvigoration of Dr. King's ideals, therefore, would be a productive first step towards universal cultural progress. In order to brainstorm strategies that may cultivate change, recognition of specific obstacles is necessary.

As the economic landscape becomes more consolidated, a small number of companies continue to acquire massive power over the market and the government. With less competition, these companies broaden their control over supply, demand, and consumer prices.

The political influence market power offers enables large corporations to obtain subsidies and promote industry friendly tax policies. Small businesses do not have these abilities, nor can they compete with the grand scale advertising of big business. The most powerful corporations lobby to encourage requirements for sales licensing, which makes it difficult for new, small businesses to penetrate a market.

Although patents provide citizens the benefit of owning an idea, in the genetic modification and pharmaceutical industries, patents give companies long-term monopolies on agricultural seeds and new drugs.[37] Water, electricity, cable and internet companies also profit immensely from varying levels of monopoly power at the excessive expense of consumers. Oligopolies, which now exist in nearly every industry, allow a few firms to maintain shared market power by operating with identical or nearly identical financial strategies, pricing agreements, and mechanisms like vertical competition fixing agreements.

When firms in an industry all charge the same rates, the prices are fixed whether or not there is public evidence of a meeting in which owners have conspired to do so.[38] However, as mentioned earlier, a Koch-controlled company has been convicted of price fixing, while Cargill has settled out of court to pay off the same accusation. Koch Industries and Cargill are the two most profitable private American corporations. Dow, one of the companies that provide an index by which the American stock market is measured, has also been found liable of price fixing. One may wonder how often such behavior is not caught.

Meanwhile, consumer food prices remain exorbitantly high and continue to rise.[39]

---

[37] In the genetic modification and pharmaceutical industries, patents are granted for a period of twenty years, although the length of time to bring a new product onto the market varies.

[38] During a speech delivered at the Springfield, Illinois Republican State Convention in 1858, Abraham Lincoln, used an architectural metaphor to describe the recognition of undocumented collusion: "When we see a lot of framed timbers, different proportions of which we know have been gotten out at different times and places by different workmen—Stephen, Franklin, Roger, and James, for instance—and when we see that these timbers joined together, and see they exactly make the frame of a house . . . all the lengths and proportions of the different pieces exactly adapted to their respective places . . . we find it impossible to not believe that Stephen and Franklin and Roger and James all understood one another from the beginning, and all worked with a common plan or draft drawn up before the first lick was struck."

[39] Abundant supply is theoretically supposed to bring costs down for consumers, but that does not always occur. To cite one example, the advent of genetic modification came with promises of higher crop yields and subsequently lower

The Federal Trade Commission (FTC), which is charged with the responsibility to "protect consumers and promote competition," has not shown the ability to do so, despite their periodic enforcement of antitrust laws. Indeed, there has not been an effective mechanism in place to ensure that American corporations pass on a reasonable percentage of profits to workers or a fair price to consumers. According to the FTC, price fixing is "almost always illegal," and "hard to uncover."

The American Legislative Exchange Council (ALEC) is a powerful pro-corporate group of lobbyists and legislators that vote on policies in private meetings and then develop procedures to promote industry-friendly laws introduced at the state level. The Council For National Policy (CNP, CFNP) operates in a similar fashion, yet with more of a clear link to a federal focus. Koch Industries is among the members of both organizations. Of course, industry leaders and legislators can discuss and implement strategies anywhere, anytime, and they do not necessarily have to be associated with ALEC or CNP. Other groups, such as the U.S. Chamber of Commerce and the Business Roundtable, represent various corporations and are consistently among the top lobbyists.

The largest companies benefit from the ability to continually increase in proportion by means of acquisitions and mergers. Size also allows for additional conditions that perpetuate growth. Economies of scale occur when a high quantity of production lowers costs on individual products. Economies of scope are acquired when a company can save on individual products by selling a greater variety.

Technological advances offer corporations the capacity to replace workers with machines, resulting in increased profit and less

---

food prices for consumers. A GAO report conducted in 2009 found that from 1982 to 2009, as we saw massive production of corn and soy—genetically modified since the early 1990s—and over-saturation of those crops into various products we consume, food prices outpaced inflation by 26%. Industry attributed this circumstance to rising fuel costs, however the market price of fuel has not fluctuated in accordance with the cost of food.

necessity to pay human employees. Expensive technology and infrastructure is only available to firms that can afford it or obtain considerable credit. Big businesses also save money on cheap foreign labor and tax havens. Although industry spokespeople often argue that giant corporations create jobs, others point out that a job is only fruitful if the wage is reasonable, and a large number of small businesses can provide the same employment as a small number of large businesses.

Yet the current economic condition finds small businesses increasingly disappearing. Those that survive and flourish become likely candidates for mergers and acquisitions. Industries grow more concentrated, competition deteriorates and consumer prices rise. Consequently, regulations, specifically on big business, are necessary to restore a "free market" and reasonable costs for the highest percentage of Americans. Such regulations need not be unnecessarily complicated.

Unfortunately, in addition to lack of funding and inadequate staff, conflicts of interest have rendered our regulatory system unsuccessful. Numerous influential employees at agencies including the FDA, the EPA, the USDA, the FTC and the SEC, have worked with or continue to invest in the industries they are responsible for regulating. Replacing those personnel with independent scientists, economists, scholars, and humanitarians would be a productive first step in implementing effective oversight. In addition, an expansive, well-funded criminal investigation into price fixing and collusion between corporations and government would reveal the potential for universal economic and regulatory improvement.

More substantial changes will be required to cultivate national well-being. Having considered a few original ideas and promising improvements suggested by others, I would like to offer a handful of possible solutions. It occurs to me that some of these ideas may seem radical, or exceedingly difficult to implement. Nevertheless, deliberation is a necessary step toward action.

A program for periodically fragmenting the largest companies into numerous small companies could consistently restore a reasonable level of healthy competition in the American market.

Such a procedure would depend on regulations that ensure no employees lose their jobs or previously acquired wealth in the process.

Reforming the patenting system to address monopolies and fragmenting the utility-based monopolies that currently exist would likewise promote competition, and consequently lower consumer costs.

Education that focuses on independent analysis and critical thinking would teach citizens to conduct objective research before believing a biased source with a special interest. Early attention to psychology, logic, tolerance, and love would reduce tyrannical behavior and instill in children the knowledge that the color of one's skin does not precipitate a specific type of behavior or code of ethics, despite cultural differences.[40] Effective education, ultimately, could lead to a public capable of electing qualified leaders that exhibit actions to prove humanitarian claims made during campaigns. Consequently, appropriate leaders could maintain a market prosperous for everyone by regulating industries or personnel detrimental to the general welfare.

Speechwriters and advisors can make an incompetent, unethical candidate appear to be a saint. If politicians were required to write

---

[40] Nelson Mandela wrote in his autobiography, "People must learn to hate, and if they can learn to hate, they can be taught to love, for love comes more naturally to the human heart than its opposite." Science has backed his philosophy. A 2013 study performed by researchers at the University of Illinois and the University of California found that an amygdala response in the human brain associated with differentiation of ethnicities does not emerge until adolescence, which suggests that prejudice develops as a learned behavior. In the same study, those raised around diverse peers had diminished amygdala responses to contrasting ethnicities.

Another recent study, funded by the Medical Research Council and published in *Nature,* concluded that children born from ethnically different parents grew taller, exhibited better cognitive skills, and reached higher education levels than those born from same-race parents, indicating that nature itself relishes diversity. Such a conclusion is not new, yet, reading the comments section beneath articles that refer to this study, one finds a surprising amount of anger and anecdotal contradiction. It seems that many people have perceived science like this to be an attempt to promote the idea that children born exclusively of white parents are somehow inept.

their own speeches, and held to rigorous legal standards of truth, then voters could more accurately perceive their merit.

Overturning the *Citizens United* decision would be constructive, but it would not change the fact that only the wealthy can compete for government office. If political contenders were required to exclusively solicit small individual donations, and disallowed to use income acquired previous to a campaign, then corporate influence would diminish, and the less wealthy would have more representatives. Low caps on spending to sway voters through the media or other means would further promote parity in influencing public policy.

If American corporations were not enabled to use offshore tax havens, then they would pay for a higher percentage of the federal budget, creating the possibility of lower taxes for the highest percentage of people.

In addition, if American companies were required to pay the American minimum wage in the foreign countries where they save on labor, they would have a financial incentive to employ domestic workers. Yet if they did operate overseas, the employees there would be fairly compensated, and friendlier foreign relations could ensue. Certainly, continuing to improve the minimum wage in America will enhance the livelihoods of the local impoverished.

Simply convicting individual executives for corporate crimes would encourage accountability.

When Dr. King arrived in Memphis to help exploited sanitation workers, he demonstrated the importance of fair compensation for labor. Statistics show that today in America, most of the upper, middle, and lower class have to work more hours to maintain the same standard of living achieved with fewer hours in the past. The reasons for this have been debated, but the most evident cause is corporate market power, concentration and lobbying, which combine to give big businesses substantial control over legislation, wages and prices. Subsequently, American consumers of various ethnicities and political persuasions suffer at the bottom of a wealth gap, while a miniscule percentage of the financial elite prosper at the top.

Among the numerous investigators and scattering of politicians that have brought this condition to public attention, *New York Times* journalist Floyd Norris used Commerce Department statistics to show that corporate profits as a percentage of gross domestic product were higher in 2014 than in at least the previous eighty-five years, while the percentage of employee compensation measured the lowest in sixty-five years. An *equal* distribution of wealth and goods is not necessary, but the concern for a *fair* distribution of wealth is legitimate.

Tolerating or accepting injustice prevents the possibility of relinquishing oppression. Responding to exploitation or hatred with violence, however, creates more violence. In such a circumstance, whoever is already most powerful will most often emerge as the victor. In contrast, responding with peaceful non-compliance diminishes the possibility of an oppressor to exert their will. If more than half of society were to react in such a manner, then the tyrannical forces that be would be pressured to concede or at least compromise. That is what Gandhi, Mandela, and King understood so well, and it might be why they were all removed from power as their influence grew. Yet there is still power in numbers. And considering that tyrants can only oppress those who allow it to happen, civil disobedience continues to be the most illuminating path to freedom.

While King's dream resounds in the minds of many, others attempt to make reasonable arguments to explain why equality is unnecessary, or harmful. Widespread economic strife remains. In addition, the 2016 presidential election indicates that America still has a long way to go in terms of curtailing racism, a condition compounded by the common legitimization of Trump.[41] [42]

---

[41] Donald Trump: "When Mexico sends its people, they're not sending the best. They're not sending you. They're not sending you. They're sending people that have lots of problems, and they're bringing those problems with us. They're bringing drugs. They're bringing crime. They're rapists. And some, I assume, are good people." Relative to population, statistics show that the United States harbors far more rapists, drug users and total criminals than Mexico. Trump's inaccurate judgments on a specific ethnicity define racism. It should also be noted that Mexico, being a geographic location, is incapable of sending anyone anywhere. Trump's claim that the "heavy Arab population" in New Jersey celebrated after the

Hope remains, however, so long as citizens deliberately pursue the quest for knowledge, progress, and fellowship. If we can teach our children to look past electronic devices, to get outside, travel and learn about different cultures; to read critically; to embrace giving and value people based on actions rather than appearance or empty words, then, in the future, we just may be able to elect representatives with the ability and desire to create a truly harmonious society in which citizens are fairly compensated for their labor, where nobody has to feel hated, and hate in return.

After the assassination, the King family spoke with James Earl Ray, as well as various authorities and witnesses to learn more about their suspicion of government involvement. Eventually, they revealed their conclusion that a government conspiracy existed to the public and were subsequently belittled by the media. When Dr. King's wife, Coretta, attempted to explain to her son the reasons for media attacks against her husband following an anti-war speech in 1967, she said: "You have to understand that when you take a stand against the establishment, first, you will be attacked. There is an attempt to discredit. Second [an attempt] to try and character-assassinate. And third, ultimately physical termination or assassination."

Yet King's message cannot be killed by a gun, nor a sword, nor the pen. May we never forget that he died to bring us the love we all need, and that the best way to be loved is to love others.

In the words of a true King, struck too soon by tragedy:

"The ultimate measure of a man is not where he stands in times of comfort and convenience, but where he stands at times of challenge and controversy."

9/11 attacks, also proven false, presents another example of ethnic misrepresentation.

[42] As recently as 2002, Republican House Majority Whip Steve Scalise gave a speech to the white supremacist European-American Unity and Rights Organization (EURO). He and eight Republicans currently (3/20/17) serving in congress have voted against acknowledging Martin Luther King Day.

"The hope of a secure and livable world lies with disciplined and dedicated nonconformists . . . set on building . . . an order of justice, peace and brotherhood."

"Take the first step in faith. You don't have to see the whole staircase, just take the first step."

"If you can't fly, run; if you can't run, walk; if you can't walk, crawl; but by all means keep moving."

"Somewhere we must come to see that human progress never rolls in on wheels of inevitability. It comes through the tireless efforts and the persistent work of dedicated individuals. Without this hard work, time becomes an ally of the primitive forces of social stagnation. So we must help time and realize that the time is always right to do right."

End

Note on Sources

After reading one book and numerous mainstream articles on King's assassination, it seemed to me that James Earl Ray took the fatal shot. Upon digging deeper, I became aware that this was not a proven fact despite it often being depicted as such. I learned of Philip Melanson (*Who Killed Martin Luther King, The Murkin Conspiracy*), William Pepper (*Orders to Kill, An Act of State*), Michael K. Honey (*Going Down Jericho Road*), and Jim Douglass (*Probe*), all of whom had done excellent work on the subject. Unfortunately, even though these particular writers were thorough and reasonable, they received little media attention.

Information from the House Select Committee on Assassinations, *King Versus Jowers and Other Unknown Co-conspirators*, and the Church Committee on Intelligence Overreach provided in depth insight. I would encourage anyone interested in the subject to explore those sources in order to ascertain critical details.

Many accounts avoid elaborating on evidence of government involvement in the assassination. One example, *Hellhound on His Trail . . .* , a nonfiction narrative by Hampton Sides that reads like fiction, does a suspenseful job of tracing many details of the manhunt, but it focuses primarily on James Earl Ray, one player in a larger picture. Sides fails to mention the time Ray spent in Canada months after his escape from the Missouri State Penitentiary, and did not explore *King v. Jowers* . . . . In addition, much of the information Sides described as truth in his book was derived from a source called the Hughes collection. Vince Hughes is an amateur archivist and former Memphis policeman who has made his collection available to less than ten people. Hughes said that many pieces in the collection cannot be found anywhere else, but he doesn't allow "folks that are looking for conspiracy and those kinds of things," to access it, even though the House Select Committee on Assassinations and *King v. Jowers* . . . both concluded a conspiracy existed. Although *Hellhound* . . . was incomplete, and contained a profusion of unverifiable information, I was able to verify some of the quotations and events therein, like the driver hoax in Memphis as well as the FBI's harassment of King. Those that I found to be authentic were included in my narrative.

Gerald Posner's book *Killing the Dream* argues that a conspiracy existed, but that it included James Earl Ray and his brothers, who never sought the $50,000 payment Posner said was their motive. The same author wrote *Case Closed*, which attempts to establish Lee Harvey Oswald as the lone culprit in John Kennedy's assassination. A lawyer by training, Gerald Posner has represented the Afghan security contractor Haji Ruhullah and family members of the former Afghan president tied to banking scandals, as well as weapons and narcotics trafficking.

Rachel Maddow broadcast an interesting segment on the John Birch Society and she has done admirable work on the Koch brothers. For additional information on the Kochs, I drew largely from Jane Mayer (*Dark Money*), among other journalists and publications including Lee Fang, *Bloomberg Markets*, and the *New Yorker*.

The Center for Responsive Politics provided valuable knowledge regarding the activities of the largest lobbyists. The CRP is an excellent source for those interested in understanding the relationships between businesses and politicians.

I acquired details on the Memphis Sanitation Strike from University of Washington professor and author Michael Honey's *Going Down Jericho Road*.

The web links https://nsa.gov1.info/surveillance/index.html and https://nsa.gov1.info/data/ in my sources do not represent the views of the NSA. Both are well-researched parodies with accurate details regarding government surveillance.

The quotations that conclude the narrative I drew from a scattering of Dr. King's speeches and writings.

Additionally, I consolidated quotations from intelligence expert William Schapp, particularly in the chapter entitled Big Brother Cracks Down on Thought Crimes, in order to remove redundancy and maintain narrative flow. The message of the content has not been manipulated in any way.

References

All sources accessed between March 2015 and May 2018.

Introduction

"Assassination Conspiracy Trial." *Thekingcenter.Org.* The King Center. Web.
http://www.thekingcenter.org/assassination-conspiracy-trial

Ratcliffe, David. "Complete Transcript of the Martin Luther King, Jr. Assassination Conspiracy Trial."
Ratical.org. Rat Haus Reality Press, Aug. 2012. Web. http://ratical.org/ratville/JFK/MLKACT/

"IV. Jowers' Allegations." *Justice.Gov.* U.S. Department of Justice. Web.
https://www.justice.gov/crt/iv-jowers-allegations

Yellin, Emily. "Memphis Jury Sees Conspiracy in Martin Luther King's Killing." *Nytimes.Com.* The
New York Times, 9 Dec. 1999. Web. http://www.nytimes.com/1999/12/09/us/memphis-jury-sees-
conspiracy-in-martin-luther-king-s-killing.html

"Intelligence Related Commissions, Other Select or Special Committees and Special Reports."
Intelligence.Senate.Gov. U.S. Senate Select Committee on Intelligence. Web.
http://www.intelligence.senate.gov/resources/intelligence-related-commissions (See Senate Select
Committee to Study Governmental Operations with Respect to Intelligence Activities, 1975-1976
[Church Committee], Book III, pg. 79.)

"HSCA Final Assassinations Report." *History-Matters.Com.* History Matters. Web.
https://www.history-matters.com/archive/contents/hsca/contents_hsca_report.htm (pg. 5, 263-460)

Chapter 1

"What Happened in 1955 Important News and Events, Key Technology and Popular Culture." *Thepeoplehistory.Com*. The People History. Web. http://www.thepeoplehistory.com/1955.html

"George Wallace, 'Segregation Now, Segregation Forever.'" *Blackpast.Org*. BlackPast.org. Web. http://www.blackpast.org/1963-george-wallace-segregation-now-segregation-forever https://www.youtube.com/watch?v=6C-kBVggFrs

"Freedom Riders. Meet the Players: Other Figures." *Pbs.Org*. PBS. Web. http://www.pbs.org/wgbh/americanexperience/features/meet-players-other-figures/

Smith, Jordan Michael. "The Republican Party's Race Problem and Strom Thurmond's Legacy." *Thedailybeast.Com*. Daily Beast, 9 Sept. 2012. Web. https://www.thedailybeast.com/the-republican-partys-race-problem-and-strom-thurmonds-legacy

Sides, Hampton. "Hellhound on His Trail . . ." New York: Anchor Books, 2011. Print.

Robinson, Eugene. "Robert Byrd: A story of change and redemption." *Washingtonpost.Com*. The Washington Post, 29 June 2010. Web. http://www.washingtonpost.com/wp-dyn/content/article/2010/06/28/AR2010062803119.html

"The FBI vs. Martin Luther King: Inside J. Edgar Hoover's 'Suicide Letter' to Civil Rights Leader." *Democracynow.Org*. Democracy Now!, 18 Nov. 2014. Web. https://www.democracynow.org/2014/11/18/the_fbi_vs_martin_luther_king

Schlesinger, Arthur M. "Robert Kennedy and His Times." New York: Mariner Books, 1978. Google Books. Web. goo.gl/PPDeFd

King, Martin Luther, Jr. "Martin Luther King Jr. - Acceptance Speech." Oslo, Norway, 10 Dec. 1964. *Nobelprize.Org*. The Nobel Foundation. Web. http://www.nobelprize.org/nobel_prizes/peace/laureates/1964/king-acceptance_en.html

Johnson, Marv. "History Repeated: The Dangers of Domestic Spying by Federal Law Enforcement." *Aclu.Org*. ACLU. Web. https://www.aclu.org/files/images/asset_upload_file893_29902.pdf

King, Martin Luther, Jr. "Beyond Vietnam." Riverside Church. New York, NY., 4 April 1967. *Kingencyclopedia.Stanford.Edu*. The King Institute. Web. http://kingencyclopedia.stanford.edu/encyclopedia/documentsentry/doc_beyond_vietnam/

King, Martin Luther, Jr. "The Domestic Impact of the War in America." National Labor Leadership Assembly for Peace. University of Chicago, Chicago, IL., 11 Nov. 1967. *Thekingcenter.Org*. The King Center. Web. http://www.thekingcenter.org/archive/document/domestic-impact-war-america

King, Martin Luther, Jr. "Remaining Awake Through a Great Revolution." National Cathedral, Washington D.C., 31 Mar. 1968. *Kingencyclopedia.Stanford.Edu.* The King Institute. Web. http://kingencyclopedia.stanford.edu/encyclopedia/documentsentry/doc_remaining_awake_through_a_great_revolution.1.html

"Martin Luther King, Jr. and the Global Freedom Struggle: Hoover, J. Edgar." *Kingencyclopedia.Stanford.Edu.* The King Institute. Web. http://kingencyclopedia.stanford.edu/encyclopedia/encyclopedia/enc_hoover_j_edgar_1895_1972/

Dreier, Peter. "This Labor Day, Remember that Martin Luther King's Last Campaign was for Workers' Rights." *Commondreams.Org.* Common Dreams, 3 Sept. 2017. Web. https://www.commondreams.org/views/2017/09/03/labor-day-remember-martin-luther-kings-last-campaign-was-workers-rights

Chapter 2

"Intelligence Related Commissions, Other Select or Special Committees and Special Reports." *Intelligence.Senate.Gov.* (Senate Select Committee to Study Governmental Operations with Respect to Intelligence Activities, 1975-1976 [Church Committee], Book III, pg. 137.)

Berman, Emily. "FBI Overreaching." *Brennancenter.Org.* Brennan Center for Justice at New York University School of Law, 8 Nov. 2010. Web. https://www.brennancenter.org/analysis/fbi-overreaching

German, Michael. "The U.S. Needs a New Church Committee." *Brennancenter.Org.* Brenan Center for Justice at New York University School of Law, 11 Dec. 2014. Web. https://www.brennancenter.org/analysis/us-needs-new-church-committee

Sides, Hampton. "Hellhound on His Trail . . ."

Griffey, Trevor. "Memphis Commercial Appeal Assisted FBI's COINTELPRO Against Black Nationalists." *Seattlepi.Com.* Seattle Post-Intelligencer, 18 Nov. 2010. Web. http://blog.seattlepi.com/trevorgriffey/2010/11/18/memphis-commercial-appeal-assisted-fbis-cointelpro-against-black-nationalists/

"Martin Luther King, Jr. and the Global Freedom Struggle: Highlander Folk School." *Kingencyclopedia.Stanford.Edu.* The King Institute. Web. http://kingencyclopedia.stanford.edu/encyclopedia/encyclopedia/enc_highlander_folk_school.1.html http://kingencyclopedia.stanford.edu/primarydocuments/650300-002.pdf

"Highlander Folk School - Image Gallery Essay." *Wisconsinhistory.Org.* Wisconsin Historical Society. Web. https://www.wisconsinhistory.org/Records/Article/CS3956

"The Beast as a Saint: The Truth About Martin Luther King, Jr." *Stormfront.Org.* Web. http://www.martinlutherking.org/thebeast.html http://www.martinlutherking.org/commie-school.html

"Assassination Conspiracy Trial." *Thekingcenter.Org.*

"Danger in Demonstrations." Chicago's American, 8 Aug. 1966. *Thekingcenter.Org.* The King Center. Web. http://thekingcenter.org/archive/document/danger-demonstrations

"Dr. King Outdated." The Charlotte News, 15 July 1967. *Thekingcenter.Org.* The King Center. Web. http://thekingcenter.org/archive/document/dr-king-outdated

"The Archive." *Thekingcenter.Org.* The King Center. Web. http://thekingcenter.org/archive

Bernstein, Carl. "The CIA and the Media." Rolling Stone, 20 Oct. 1977. *Carlbernstein.Com.* Web. http://www.carlbernstein.com/magazine_cia_and_media.php

Hersh, Seymour M. "Huge C.I.A. Operation Reported In U.S. Against Antiwar Forces, Other Dissidents In Nixon Years." The New York Times, 22 Dec. 1974. *Documentcloud.Org.* http://www.documentcloud.org/documents/238963-huge-c-i-a-operation-reported-in-u-s-against.html

"Operation Chaos . . ." The New York Times, 11 June 1975. *Nytimes.Com.* Web. http://www.nytimes.com/1975/06/11/archives/operation-chaos.html

Upano, Alicia. "Will a History of Government Using Journalists Repeat Itself Under the Department of Homeland Security?" *Rcfp.Org.* The News Media and the Law, Winter 2003. Web. http://www.rcfp.org/browse-media-law-resources/news-media-law/news-media-and-law-winter-2003/will-history-government-usi

Chapter 3

Garrow, David J. "The FBI and Martin Luther King." *Theatlantic.Com.* The Atlantic, July 2002. Web. http://www.theatlantic.com/magazine/archive/2002/07/the-fbi-and-martin-luther-king/302537/

Sides, Hampton. "Hellhound . . ." (pg. 38, 39, 68)

Schlesinger, Arthur M. "Robert Kennedy and His Times." New York: Mariner Books, 1978. (pg. 260) Google Books. Web. goo.gl/PPDeFd

Gage, Beverly. "What an Uncensored Letter to M.L.K. Reveals." *Nytimes.Com.* The New York Times, 11 Nov. 2014. Web. http://www.nytimes.com/2014/11/16/magazine/what-an-uncensored-letter-to-mlk-reveals.html?_r=0

Thompson, Catherine. "Revealed: FBI Allegedly Tried to Persuade MLK to Kill Himself Over Threatened Sex Stories." *Businessinsider.Com.* Business Insider, 12 Nov. 2014. Web. http://www.businessinsider.com/shocking-letter-from-fbi-to-martin-luther-king-2014-11

"Williams, Jennie Celeste Parks." *Kingencyclopedia.Stanford.Edu.* The King Institute. Web.

http://kingencyclopedia.stanford.edu/encyclopedia/encyclopedia/enc_williams_jennie_celeste_parks_1873_1941/

Chapter 4

Sides, Hampton.

"Muhammad Ali Refuses to Fight in Vietnam War." *Theguardian.Com*. The Guardian, 29 April 1967. https://www.theguardian.com/theguardian/2013/apr/29/muhammad-ali-refuses-to-fight-in-vietnam-war-1967

Sergeant, John and John Edginton. "The Conspiracy to Kill Martin Luther King." *Chicagoreader.Com*. Chicago Reader, 1 Mar. 1990. Web. http://www.chicagoreader.com/chicago/the-conspiracy-to-kill-martin-luther-king/Content?oid=875281

Nicol, John. "Canadian Connection in the Martin Luther King Assassination." *Cbc.Ca*. CBC News, 28 April 2008. Web. http://www.cbc.ca/news/world/canadian-connection-in-the-martin-luther-king-assassination-1.696100

"James Earl Ray Biography." *Notablebiographies.Com*. Encyclopedia of World Biography. Web. http://www.notablebiographies.com/supp/Supplement-Mi-So/Ray-James-Earl.html

Chapter 5

King, Martin Luther, Jr. "'I Have a Dream' Address Delivered at the March on Washington for Jobs and Freedom." Lincoln Memorial, Washington D.C., 28 Aug. 1963. *Kinginstitute.Stanford.Edu*. The King Institute. Web. https://kinginstitute.stanford.edu/king-papers/documents/i-have-dream-address-delivered-march-washington-jobs-and-freedom

King, Martin Luther, Jr. "Strength to Love." *Thekingcenter.Org*. The King Center. Web. (Pg.37) http://www.thekingcenter.org/archive/document/strength-love

"Poor People's Campaign." *Kingencyclopedia.Stanford.Edu*. The King Institute. Web. http://kingencyclopedia.stanford.edu/encyclopedia/encyclopedia/enc_poor_peoples_campaign/

Honey, Michael K. "Going Down Jericho Road: The Memphis Strike, Martin Luther King's Last Campaign." New York: W.W. Norton & Company, 2008. Print.

"Michael Honey: Dr. Martin Luther King, Jr. and the Memphis Strike (Interview)." *Historynewsnetwork.Org*. History News Network. Web. http://historynewsnetwork.org/article/37086

Sides, Hampton.

"Memphis Sanitation Workers Strike (1968)" *Kingencyclopedia.Stanford.Edu.* The King Institute. Web. http://kingencyclopedia.stanford.edu/encyclopedia/encyclopedia/enc_memphis_sanitation_workers_strike_1968/

"At the River I Stand (Film Transcript)." *Newsreel.Org.* California Newsreel. Web. http://www.newsreel.org/transcripts/At-the-River-I-Stand-Transcript.html

King, Martin Luther, Jr. "Letter From A Birmingham Jail." Birmingham, AL, 16 Apr. 1963. *Kinginstitute.Stanford.Edu.* The King Institute. Web. https://kinginstitute.stanford.edu/king-papers/documents/letter-birmingham-jail

"Assassination Conspiracy Trial." *Thekingcenter.Org.*

Griffey, Trevor. "Memphis Commercial Appeal Assisted FBI's COINTELPRO Against Black Nationalists." *Seattlepi.Com.* Seattle Post-Intelligencer, 18 Nov. 2010. Web. http://blog.seattlepi.com/trevorgriffey/2010/11/18/memphis-commercial-appeal-assisted-fbis-cointelpro-against-black-nationalists/

Chapter 6

Sides, Hampton.

Honey, Michael. "Going Down Jericho Road."

Douglass, Jim. "The Martin Luther King Conspiracy Exposed in Memphis." Probe Magazine, Spring 2000. *Ratical.Org.* Rat Haus Reality Press. Web. http://www.ratical.org/ratville/JFK/Unspeakable/MLKconExp.html

Garrow, David. "Bearing the Cross: Martin Luther King, Jr., and the Southern Christian Leadership Conference." New York: Harper Collins, 2004. Google Books. Web.

Branch, Taylor. "At Canaan's Edge: America in the King Years, 1965-68." New York: Simon & Schuster, 2006. Google Books. Web.

"Assassination Conspiracy Trial." *Thekingcenter.Org.*

"Findings on MLK Assassination." *Archives.Gov.* The U.S. National Archives and Records Administration. Web. https://www.archives.gov/research/jfk/select-committee-report/part-2d.html

"Attorney General File." *Register.Shelby.Tn.Us.* Shelby County Register of Deeds. Web. http://register.shelby.tn.us/media/mlk/index.php?album=Attorney+General+File

"Statement of Edward E. Redditt." *Register.Shelby.Tn.Us.* Shelby County Register of Deeds, 10 Apr. 1968. Web.

http://register.shelby.tn.us/media/mlk/mlkviewimage.php?imgtype=pdf&image=ray_material_2011-02-08/attorney_general_file/microfilm_images/001438ag11.tif#

Roberts, Hannah. "Finally Revealed After 44 Years: . . ." *Dailymail.Co.Uk.* Daily Mail, 14 Jan. 2014. Web.
http://www.dailymail.co.uk/news/article-2086676/Martin-Luther-King-Jr-assassination-Rarely-seen-pictures-captured-night.html

Melanson, Philip H. "The Martin Luther King Assassination." Charlotte: S.P.I. Books, 1994. Google Books. Web. (pg. 86)

"Statement of W.B. Richmond." *Register.Shelby.Tn.Us.* Shelby County Register of Deeds, 9 Apr. 1968. Web.
http://register.shelby.tn.us/media/mlk/mlkviewimage.php?imgtype=pdf&image=ray_material_2011-02-08/attorney_general_file/microfilm_images/001479ag11.tif#

"Statement of George W. Loenneke." *Register.Shelby.Tn.Us.* Shelby County Register of Deeds, 13 Apr. 1968. Web.
http://register.shelby.tn.us/media/mlk/mlkviewimage.php?imgtype=pdf&image=ray_material_2011-02-08/attorney_general_file/microfilm_images/001311ag11.tif#

Phung, An. "Restored Videos Show James Earl Ray on Trial For Martin Luther King Assassination." *Nbcbayarea.Com.* NBC, 3 Apr. 2013. Web.
goo.gl/MfDvwi

"Michael Honey: Dr. Martin Luther King, Jr. and the Memphis Strike (Interview)." *Historynewsnetwork.Org.*

Sergeant, John and John Edginton. "The Conspiracy to Kill Martin Luther King."
https://www.chicagoreader.com/chicago/the-conspiracy-to-kill-martin-luther-king/Content?oid=875281

DiEugenio, James. "Eyewitness to Murder: The King Assassination." *Kennedysandking.Com.* Kennedys and King, 29 Nov. 2008. Web.
https://kennedysandking.com/martin-luther-king-reviews/eyewitness-to-murder-the-king-assassination

Newton, Michael. "The FBI Encyclopedia." Jefferson: McFarland & Company Inc., 2012. Google Books. Web. goo.gl/g9AQMp

Chapter 7

"Heroes and Villains: Reaction From World Leaders to the Death of King, reported in the Daily Telegraph Newspaper, 6 April 1968." *Nationalarchives.Gov.Uk.* The National Archives (UK). Web.
http://www.nationalarchives.gov.uk/education/heroesvillains/transcript/g6cs4s3t.htm

Sides, Hampton.

"Martin Luther King, Jr. Quotes III." *Notable-quotes.Com.* Notable Quotes. Web. http://www.notable-quotes.com/k/king_jr_martin_luther_iii.html

Whitaker, Morgan. "Back in the Day: What Critics Said About King's Speech in 1963." *Msnbc.Com.* MSNBC, 28 Aug. 2013. Web.
http://www.msnbc.com/msnbc/back-the-day-what-critics-said-about-king

Mays, Benjamin E. "Born to Rebel: An Autobiography." Athens: University of Georgia Press, 2003. Google Books. Web. goo.gl/nEdkp3

"Assassination Conspiracy Trial." *Thekingcenter.Org.*

Behnken, Brian B. "The Struggle in Black and Brown . . ." University of Nebraska Press, 2012. Google Books. Web. goo.gl/BQk36t

Johnson, Bill. "LBJ Delays Hawaii Trip." The Day, 5 Apr. 1968. Google News. Web.
https://news.google.com/newspapers?nid=1915&dat=19810404&id=XgEhAAAAIBAJ&sjid=_nQFAA AAIBAJ&pg=2836,770184&hl=en

"Michael Honey: Dr. Martin Luther King, Jr. and the Memphis Strike (Interview)." *Historynewsnetwork.Org.*

Honey, Michael. "Going Down Jericho Road."

Turner, April O. "Remembering Trayvon Martin: A Death That Brought a Movement to Life." *Huffingtonpost.Com.* HuffPost, 26 Feb. 2016. Web.
https://www.huffingtonpost.com/aprill-o-turner/remembering-trayvon-martin_b_9328256.html

Chapter 8

Sides, Hampton.

Sergeant, John and John Edginton. "The Conspiracy to Kill Martin Luther King."

"HSCA Final Assassinations Report." (pg. 5, 263-460) *History-Matters.Com.*

"Findings on MLK Assassination." *Archives.Gov.* The U.S. National Archives and Records Administration. Web.
https://www.archives.gov/research/jfk/select-committee-report/part-2a.html

"Bobby Hutton." *Pbs.Org.* PBS. Web.
http://www.pbs.org/hueypnewton/people/people_hutton.html

Pease, Lisa. "Martin Luther King's Son Says: James Earl Ray Didn't Kill MLK!" *Realhistoryarchives.Com.* Probe Magazine, May-June 1997. Web.
http://www.realhistoryarchives.com/collections/assassinations/pr597-mlk-full.html

Nicol, John. "Canadian Connection in the Martin Luther King Assassination." *Cbc.Ca.* CBC News, 28 April 2008. Web.
http://www.cbc.ca/news/world/canadian-connection-in-the-martin-luther-king-assassination-1.696100

"James Earl Ray Biography." *Notablebiographies.Com.* Encyclopedia of World Biography. Web.
http://www.notablebiographies.com/supp/Supplement-Mi-So/Ray-James-Earl.html

"Martin Luther King Jr.'s Assassin FBI Wanted Posters 442 & 442A April 17/19, 1968." *Hakes.Com.* Hake's Americana & Collectibles. Web.
https://www.hakes.com/Auction/ItemDetail/79595/MARTIN-LUTHER-KING-JRs-ASSASSIN-FBI-WANTED-POSTERS-442-442A-APRIL-1719-1968

Chapter 9

Cho, Nancy. "Poor People's Campaign (December 4, 1967 - June 19, 1968)." *Blackpast.Org.* BlackPast.org. Web.
http://www.blackpast.org/aah/poor-peoples-campaign-december-4-1967-june-19-1968

Franklin, Ben A. "5,000 Open Poor People's Campaign in Washington." *Nytimes.Com.* The New York Times, 13 May 1968. Web.
http://query.nytimes.com/gst/abstract.html?res=9803EEDB163AE134BC4B52DFB3668383679EDE&url=&legacy=true

"Poor People's Campaign." *Kingencyclopedia.Stanford.Edu.* The King Institute. Web.
http://kingencyclopedia.stanford.edu/encyclopedia/encyclopedia/enc_poor_peoples_campaign/

Sides, Hampton.

Black, George. "The Lethal Legacy of the Vietnam War." *Thenation.Com.* The Nation, 25 Feb. 2015. Web.
https://www.thenation.com/article/lethal-legacy-vietnam-war/

Dillingham, Jon. "Vietnam: Chemical Companies, US Authorities Knew the Dangers of Agent Orange." *Europe-solidaire.Org.* Europe Solidaire Sans Frontieres, 10 Aug. 2009. Web.
http://www.europe-solidaire.org/spip.php?article14706

T.M., Hang Thai. "Agent Orange, Exposed: How U.S. Chemical Warfare in Vietnam Unleashed a Slow-Moving Disaster." *Theconversation.Com.* The Conversation, 3 Oct. 2017. Web.
http://theconversation.com/agent-orange-exposed-how-u-s-chemical-warfare-in-vietnam-unleashed-a-slow-moving-disaster-84572

"Agent Orange: Background on Monsanto's Involvement." *Monsanto.Com.* Monsanto, 7 Apr. 2017. Web.
https://monsanto.com/company/media/statements/agent-orange-background/

"Agent Orange." *Dow.Com*. Dow. Web.
https://www.dow.com/en-us/about-dow/issues-and-challenges/agent-orange

Chapter 10

"Corporate Crime and Abuse: Tracking the Problem." *Corporatepolicy.Org*. Center for Corporate Policy. Web.
http://www.corporatepolicy.org/issues/crimedata.htm

Bonn, Scott A. "Greedy Elite Criminals Get Away With 'Murder.'" *Psychologytoday.Com*. Psychology Today, 10 Mar. 2014. Web.
https://www.psychologytoday.com/blog/wicked-deeds/201403/greedy-elite-criminals-get-away-murder

"2016 Crime Statistics Released." *Fbi.Gov*. U.S. Department of Justice. Web.
https://www.fbi.gov/news/stories/2016-crime-statistics-released

"2014 Crime in the United States." *Fbi.Gov*. U.S. Department of Justice. Web.
https://www.fbi.gov/news/stories/latest-crime-stats-released

"2014 Crime in the United States: Table 23, Offense Analysis." *Fbi.Gov*. U.S. Department of Justice. Web.
https://ucr.fbi.gov/crime-in-the-u.s/2014/crime-in-the-u.s.-2014/tables/table-23

Winslow, George. "Capital Crimes: The Political Economy of Crime in America." *Monthlyreview.Org*. Monthly Review, 01 Nov. 2000. Web.
https://monthlyreview.org/2000/11/01/capital-crimes/

Wouters, Jorgen. "One in Four Households Victim of White Collar Crime: Report." *Aol.Com*. AOL, 13 Dec. 2010. Web.
https://www.aol.com/2010/12/13/one-in-4-households-victim-of-white-collar-crime-report/

Mokhiber, Russell. "20 Things You Should Know About Corporate Crime." *Hlrecord.Org*. The Harvard Law Record, 24 Mar. 2015. Web.
http://hlrecord.org/2015/03/20-things-you-should-know-about-corporate-crime/

Light, Donald W. "New Prescription Drugs: A Major Health Risk With Few Offsetting Advantages." *Ethics.Harvard.Edu*. Harvard: Edmond J. Safra Center for Ethics, 27 June 2014. Web.
https://ethics.harvard.edu/blog/new-prescription-drugs-major-health-risk-few-offsetting-advantages

Light, Donald W. and Lexchin, Joel and Darrow, Jonathan J. "Institutional Corruption of Pharmaceuticals and the Myth of Safe and Effective Drugs" (June 1, 2013). *Papers.Ssrn.Com*. Journal of Law, Medicine and Ethics, 2013, Vol. 14, No. 3: 590-610. Web.
https://ssrn.com/abstract=2282014

Cha, Ariana Eunjung. "Researchers: Medical Errors Now Third Leading Cause of Death in United States." *Washingtonpost.Com*. The Washington Post, 3 May 2016. Web.

https://www.washingtonpost.com/news/to-your-health/wp/2016/05/03/researchers-medical-errors-now-third-leading-cause-of-death-in-united-states/?utm_term=.ffabd39c76b9

Makary Martin A. and Daniel Michael. "Medical error—the third leading cause of death in the US." *BMJ* 2016; 353 :i2139. Bmj.Com. BMJ Publishing Group Ltd, 3 May 2016. http://www.bmj.com/content/353/bmj.i2139

"Top Spenders." *Opensecrets.Org.* The Center for Responsive Politics. Web. https://www.opensecrets.org/lobby/top.php?indexType=s

Anderson, Richard. "Pharmaceutical Industry Gets High on Fat Profits." *Bbc.Com.* BBC, 6 Nov. 2014. Web. http://www.bbc.com/news/business-28212223

"Fatal Occupational Injuries by Selected Characteristics . . ." *Bls.Gov.* U.S. Bureau of Labor Statistics. Web. https://www.bls.gov/iif/oshwc/cfoi/cftb0186.pdf

Krantz, David S. "How Stress Affects Your Health." *Apa.Org.* American Psychological Association. Web. http://www.apa.org/helpcenter/stress.aspx

Caiazzo, Fabio. "Air Pollution and Early Deaths in the United States. Part I: Quantifying the Impact of Major Sectors in 2005." *Sciencedirect.Com.* Atmospheric Environment, Volume 79, Nov. 2013. Web. https://www.sciencedirect.com/science/article/pii/S1352231013004548

University of Manchester. "Scientists Suggest that Cancer is Purely Man-made." *Medicalxpress.Com.* Medical Xpress, 14 Oct. 2010. Web. https://medicalxpress.com/news/2010-10-scientists-cancer-purely-man-made.html

"Known and Probable Human Carcinogens." *Cancer.Org.* American Cancer Society, 3 Nov. 2016. Web. https://www.cancer.org/cancer/cancer-causes/general-info/known-and-probable-human-carcinogens.html

"Crime in the United States, 2000." *Archives.Fbi.Gov.* U.S. Department of Justice. Web. https://archives.fbi.gov/archives/news/pressrel/press-releases/crime-in-the-united-states-2000

"Crime in the United States, 2001." *Archives.Fbi.Gov.* U.S. Department of Justice. Web. https://archives.fbi.gov/archives/news/pressrel/press-releases/crime-in-the-united-states-2001-1

Mattera, Philip. "The 160 Billion Bank Fee." *Goodjobsfirst.Org.* Good Jobs First, June 2016. Web. http://www.goodjobsfirst.org/sites/default/files/docs/pdf/160billionbankfee.pdf

Mattera, Philip. "BP and its Brethren." *Goodjobsfirst.Org.* Good Jobs First, Oct. 2015. Web. http://www.goodjobsfirst.org/sites/default/files/docs/pdf/bpanditsbrethren.pdf

"Violation Tracker." *Goodjobsfirst.Org.* Good Jobs First. Web.
https://www.goodjobsfirst.org/violation-tracker

Mattera, Philip. "Monsanto: Corporate Rap Sheet." *Corp-research.Org.* Corporate Research Project. Web.
http://www.corp-research.org/monsanto

"Brazil Court Convicts Monsanto for False Advertising of GM Soy and Glyphosate." *Gmwatch.Org.* GMWatch, 22 Aug. 2012. Web.
http://www.gmwatch.org/en/latest-listing/51-2012/14142-brazil-court-convicts-monsanto-for-false-advertising-of-gm-soy-and-glyphosate

Associated Press. "$700 Million Settlement in Alabama PCB Lawsuit." *Nytimes.Com.* The New York Times, 21 Aug. 2003. Web.
http://www.nytimes.com/2003/08/21/business/700-million-settlement-in-alabama-pcb-lawsuit.html

"Monsanto Guilty in 'False Ad' Row." *News.Bbc.Co.Uk.* BBC, 15 Oct. 2009. Web.
http://news.bbc.co.uk/2/hi/europe/8308903.stm

"2016 Congressional Report Card on Corporate Accountability." *Earthrights.Org.* Earth Rights International. Web.
https://earthrights.org/publication/2016-congressional-report-card-on-corporate-accountability/

"The Corporate Accountability Coalition 2014 Report Card." *Earthrights.Org.* The Corporate Accountability Coalition. Web.
https://earthrights.org/wp-content/uploads/2014_cac_report_card-digital.pdf

"The Corporate Accountability Coalition 2016 Report Card." *Earthrights.Org.* The Corporate Accountability Coalition. Web.
https://earthrights.org/wp-content/uploads/2016_cac_report_card.pdf

Stewart, James B. "In Corporate Crimes, Individual Accountability is Elusive." *Nytimes.com.* The New York Times, 19 Feb. 2015. Web.
https://www.nytimes.com/2015/02/20/business/in-corporate-crimes-individual-accountability-is-elusive.html?_r=0

"U.S. Prosecution of Corporate Crime Varies Widely by Location, Program and Agency." *Trac.Syr.Edu.* Transactional Records Access Clearinghouse. Web.
http://trac.syr.edu/tracreports/crim/411/

"Cases and Proceedings." *Ftc.Gov.* Federal Trade Commission. Web.
https://www.ftc.gov/enforcement/cases-proceedings

"What We Do." *Sec.Gov.* U.S. Securities and Exchange Commission. Web.
https://www.sec.gov/Article/whatwedo.html

"U.S. -Egypt Business Council Member Companies." *Usegyptcouncil.Org*. U.S. -Egypt Business Council. Web.
http://www.usegyptcouncil.org/member-companies/ https://www.usegyptcouncil.org/about/
https://www.uschamber.com/international/middle-east-and-turkey/us-egypt-business-council

Fang, Lee. "Exclusive: Chamber Receives at Least $885,000 From Over 80 Foreign Companies in Disclosed Donations Alone." *Thinkprogress.Org*. Think Progress, 13 Oct. 2010. Web.
http://thinkprogress.org/politics/2010/10/13/123868/chamber-foreign-funded-media/

Lipton, Eric and Mike McIntire and Don Van Natta Jr. "Top Corporations Aid U.S. Chamber of Commerce Campaign." *Nytimes.Com*. The New York Times, 21 Oct. 2010. Web.
http://www.nytimes.com/2010/10/22/us/politics/22chamber.html?pagewanted=3&_r=0

Fang, Lee. "Revealed: More Corporate Donations to the U.S. Chamber's Partisan Attack Fund." *Thinkprogress.Org*. Think Progress, 22 Oct. 2010. Web.
https://thinkprogress.org/revealed-more-corporate-donations-to-the-u-s-chambers-partisan-attack-fund-44f605df54aa/

Palazzo, Chuck. "John Bachmann, Monsanto Board Member, Hides Position From US Chamber of Commerce." *Veteranstodayarchives.Com*. Veterans Today, 21 Oct. 2010. Web.
goo.gl/JyVoTQ https://goo.gl/wwdiZ7

"Membership." *Uschamber.Com*. U.S. Chamber of Commerce. Web.
https://www.uschamber.com/membership-0

Allen, Mike and Jim Vandehei. "The Koch Brothers' Secret Bank." *Politico.Com*. Politico, 11 Sept. 2013. Web.
https://www.politico.com/story/2013/09/behind-the-curtain-exclusive-the-koch-brothers-secret-bank-096669

"Brett D. Begemann." *Monsanto.Com*. Monsanto. Web.
https://monsanto.com/company/leadership/brett-d-begemann/

"Who Owns the Media?" *Pbs.Org*. PBS. Web.
http://www.pbs.org/independentlens/democracyondeadline/mediaownership.html

Lutz, Ashley. "These 6 Corporations Control 90% of the Media in America." *Businessinsider.Com*. Business Insider, 14 June 2012. Web.
http://www.businessinsider.com/these-6-corporations-control-90-of-the-media-in-america-2012-6

Harkinson, Josh. "Ever Wonder Why Your Local TV News Stations Run the Same Damn Stories?" *Motherjones.Com*. Mother Jones, 4 Apr. 2014. Web.
https://www.motherjones.com/media/2014/04/fcc-pew-local-tv-news-consolidation/

Timberg, Craig and Barton Gellman. "NSA Paying U.S. Companies for Access to Communications Networks." *Washingtonpost.Com*. The Washington Post, 29 Aug. 2013. Web.

https://www.washingtonpost.com/world/national-security/nsa-paying-us-companies-for-access-to-communications-networks/2013/08/29/5641a4b6-10c2-11e3-bdf6-e4fc677d94a1_story.html?utm_term=.0655380ffb05

"Surveillance Techniques: How Your Data Becomes Our Data." *Nsa.Gov1.Info*. Domestic Surveillance Directorate. Web.
https://nsa.gov1.info/surveillance/index.html

"Your Data: If You Have Nothing to Hide, You Have Nothing to Fear." *Nsa.Gov1.Info*. Domestic Surveillance Directorate. Web.
https://nsa.gov1.info/data/

Schneier, Bruce. "NSA Surveillance: A Guide to Staying Secure." *Theguardian.com*. The Guardian, 6 Sept. 2013. Web.
https://www.theguardian.com/world/2013/sep/05/nsa-how-to-remain-secure-surveillance

Savage, Charlie. "Obama Administration Set to Expand Sharing of Data That N.S.A. Intercepts." *Nytimes.Com*. The New York Times, 25 Feb. 2016. Web.
https://www.nytimes.com/2016/02/26/us/politics/obama-administration-set-to-expand-sharing-of-data-that-nsa-intercepts.html

Balko, Radley. "Surprise! NSA Data Will Soon Routinely be Used for Domestic Policing That has Nothing to do With Terrorism." *Washingtonpost.Com*. The Washington Post, 10 Mar. 2016. Web.
https://www.washingtonpost.com/news/the-watch/wp/2016/03/10/surprise-nsa-data-will-soon-routinely-be-used-for-domestic-policing-that-has-nothing-to-do-with-terrorism/

Kayyali, Dia. "How the NSA is Transforming Law Enforcement." *Eff.Org*. Electronic Frontier Foundation, 20 May 2014. Web.
https://www.eff.org/deeplinks/2014/05/how-nsa-transforming-law-enforcement

Kelly, John. "Cellphone Data Spying: It's Not Just the NSA." *Usatoday.Com*. USA Today. Web.
http://www.usatoday.com/story/news/nation/2013/12/08/cellphone-data-spying-nsa-police/3902809/

Eaton, Joshua. "NSA Data-Sharing Plan Opens Door to Mass Surveillance, Say Rights Groups." *Csmonitor.Com*. The Christian Science Monitor, 7 Apr. 2016. Web.
https://www.csmonitor.com/World/Passcode/2016/0407/NSA-data-sharing-plan-opens-door-to-mass-surveillance-say-rights-groups

Jouvenal, Justin. "The New Way Police Are Surveilling You: Calculating Your Threat 'Score.'" *Washingtonpost.Com*. The Washington Post, 10 Jan. 2016. Web.
https://www.washingtonpost.com/local/public-safety/the-new-way-police-are-surveilling-you-calculating-your-threat-score/2016/01/10/e42bccac-8e15-11e5-baf4-bdf37355da0c_story.html?utm_term=.2d35f02d7bb3

Friedersdorf, Conor. "Eyes Over Compton: How Police Spied on a Whole City." *Theatlantic.com*. The Atlantic, 21 Apr. 2014. Web.

http://www.theatlantic.com/national/archive/2014/04/sheriffs-deputy-compares-drone-surveillance-of-compton-to-big-brother/360954/

Berman, Emily. "FBI Overreaching." *Brennancenter.Org*. Brennan Center for Justice at New York University School of Law, 8 Nov. 2010. Web.
https://www.brennancenter.org/analysis/fbi-overreaching

German, Michael. "The U.S. Needs a New Church Committee." *Brennancenter.Org*. Brenan Center for Justice at New York University School of Law, 11 Dec. 2014. Web.
https://www.brennancenter.org/analysis/us-needs-new-church-committee

Chapter 11

Sides, Hampton.

Sergeant, John and John Edginton. "The Conspiracy to Kill Martin Luther King."

Detective Chief Inspector K. Thompson. "James Earl Ray Scotland Yard Report." *Paperlessarchives.Com*. BACM Research. Web.
http://www.paperlessarchives.com/FreeTitles/SYRayFile.pdf

Graham, Fred P. "Suspect in Assassination of Dr. King is Seized in London." *Archive.Nytimes.Com*. The New York Times, 6 June 1968. Web.
http://www.nytimes.com/learning/general/onthisday/big/0608.html

"Assassination Conspiracy Trial." *Thekingcenter.Org*.

Pianin, Eric. "A Senator's Shame." *Washingtonpost.Com*. The Washington Post, 19 June 2005. Web.
http://www.washingtonpost.com/wp-dyn/content/article/2005/06/18/AR2005061801105_pf.html

Douglass, Jim. "The Martin Luther King Conspiracy Exposed in Memphis." *Ratical.Org*. Rat Haus Reality Press. Probe Magazine, Spring 2000. Web.
http://www.ratical.org/ratville/JFK/Unspeakable/MLKconExp.html

Chapter 12

Sides, Hampton.

"Assassination Conspiracy Trial." *Thekingcenter.Org*.

"Findings on Martin Luther King, Jr. Assassination." *Archives.Gov*. The U.S. National Archives and Records Administration. Web.
https://www.archives.gov/research/jfk/select-committee-report/part-2b.html#alton (pg. 342)

Posner, Gerald. "Excerpt from Killing the Dream . . ." New York: Random House, 1998. *Washingtonpost.Com.* The Washington Post, Special Feature From Newsweek. Web. http://www.washingtonpost.com/wp-srv/national/longterm/mlk/memphis/memphis3.htm

Pepper, William. "Orders to Kill . . ." New York: Skyhorse Publishing, 1995. Google Books. Web. goo.gl/gpAK92

DiEugenio, James. "Eyewitness to Murder: The King Assassination." *Kennedysandking.Com.* Kennedys and King, 29 Nov. 2008. Web. https://kennedysandking.com/martin-luther-king-reviews/eyewitness-to-murder-the-king-assassination

Polk, James. "Officials Suspect Illinois Robbery Bankrolled Ray." *Cnn.Com.* CNN, 29 Dec. 2008. Web. http://www.cnn.com/2008/US/03/31/mlk.ray.money/index.html

Rawls, Wendell. "Probers May Criticize FBI. Likely Finding: Ray Killed King." Lawrence Journal-World, 17 Nov. 1978. N.Y. Times News Service. Google News. Web. https://news.google.com/newspapers?nid=2199&dat=19781117&id=x4QyAAAAIBAJ&sjid=zOYFAA AAIBAJ&pg=6468,3481335&hl=en

Cray, Charlie. "Halliburton." *Corpwatch.Org.* CorpWatch. Web. http://www.corpwatch.org/section.php?id=15

Holan, Angie. "Halliburton, KBR, and Iraq War Contracting: A History so Far." *Politifact.Com.* Tampa Bay Times, 9 June 2010. Web. http://www.politifact.com/truth-o-meter/statements/2010/jun/09/arianna-huffington/halliburton-kbr-and-iraq-war-contracting-history-s/

St. Clair, Jeffrey. "The Making of Halliburton." *Counterpunch.Org.* CounterPunch, 14 July 2005. Web. http://www.counterpunch.org/2005/07/14/the-making-of-halliburton/

"Autopsy Confirms Ray Died of Liver Failure." *Cnn.Com.* CNN, 24 Apr. 1998. Web. http://www.cnn.com/US/9804/24/ray.autopsy.pm/

Chapter 13

"HSCA Final Assassinations Report." *History-Matters.Com.* (pg. 5, 263-460)

Suggs, Ernie. "A.D. King Remembered on Brother's Holiday." *Ajc.Com.* The Atlanta Journal-Constitution, 16 Jan. 2014. http://www.ajc.com/news/local/king-remembered-brother-holiday/5fuH7vPgve1cTPKzYpGbhO/

Winchester, Simon. "Martin Luther King's Mother Slain in Church." *Theguardian.Com.* The Guardian, 1 July 1974. Web. https://www.theguardian.com/world/2014/jul/01/martin-luther-kings-mother-slain-in-church-1974

"Assassination Conspiracy Trial." *Thekingcenter.Org.*

Douglass, Jim. "The Martin Luther King Conspiracy Exposed in Memphis." *Ratical.Org.*

Sergeant, John and John Edginton. "The Conspiracy to Kill Martin Luther King." *Chicagoreader.Com.*

Dowd, Vincent. "Seeking Answers on King's Killer." *News.Bbc.Co.Uk.* BBC, 4 Apr. 2008. Web.
http://news.bbc.co.uk/2/hi/americas/7329763.stm

Chapter 14

"Assassination Conspiracy Trial." *Thekingcenter.Org.* (1380, 541; Young and Brown testimony.)

Chapter 15

Porter, Robert. "Contract Claims Against the Federal Government: Sovereign Immunity and Contractual Remedies." *Law.Harvard.Edu.* Harvard Law School, 2 May 2006. Web.
http://www.law.harvard.edu/faculty/hjackson/ContractClaims_22.pdf

Lobato, John and Jeffrey Theodore. "The Scope of Sovereign Immunity." *Law.Harvard.Edu.* Harvard Law School, 14 May 2006. Web.
http://www.law.harvard.edu/faculty/hjackson/FedSovereign_21.pdf

Jackson, Vicki C. "Suing the Federal Government: Sovereignty, Immunity, and Judicial Independence." *Scholarship.Law.Georgetown.Edu.* Georgetown University Law Center, 2003. Web.
https://scholarship.law.georgetown.edu/cgi/viewcontent.cgi?referer=&httpsredir=1&article=1111&context=facpub

Sisk, Gregory C. "The Continuing Drift of Federal Sovereign Immunity Jurisprudence." *Scholarship.Law.Wm.Edu.* William and Mary Law Review, Vol. 50, Issue 2, 2008.
http://scholarship.law.wm.edu/cgi/viewcontent.cgi?article=1060&context=wmlr

"Sovereign Immunity." *Legal-Dictionary.Thefreedictionary.Com.* The Free Dictionary by Farlex. Web.
http://legal-dictionary.thefreedictionary.com/Sovereign+Immunity

Douglass, Jim. "The Martin Luther King Conspiracy Exposed in Memphis."

"Assassination Conspiracy Trial." *Thekingcenter.Org.*

Pepper, William. "An Act of State." London: Verso, 2003. Google Books. Web. goo.gl/F7V6t8

Chapter 16

Douglass, Jim. "The Martin Luther King Conspiracy Exposed in Memphis."

"Civil Case: King Family Versus Jowers." (Excerpt) *Thekingcenter.Org.* The King Center. Web.
http://www.thekingcenter.org/civil-case-king-family-versus-jowers

"Assassination Conspiracy Trial." *Thekingcenter.Org.*

Sergeant, John and John Edginton. "The Conspiracy to Kill Martin Luther King." *Chicagoreader.Com.*

Pepper, William. "An Act of State." London: Verso, 2003. Google Books. Web. goo.gl/F7V6t8

Melanson, Philip H. "The Martin Luther King Assassination." Charlotte: S.P.I. Books, 1994. Google
Books. Web.
https://goo.gl/DxUJjG https://goo.gl/BRx45p

Chapter 17

Berman, Eliza. "The Photograph that Captured the Horror of MLK's Assassination." *Time.Com.* Time,
3 Apr. 2015. Web.
http://time.com/3749091/mlk-assassination-photograph/

"Joseph Louw Pictures and Images." *Gettyimages.Com.* Getty Images. Web.
https://goo.gl/PW3eaU

"The Scene of the Assassination." Pepper, William. "Orders to Kill . . ." *Ratical.Org.* Rat Haus Reality
Press. Web.
http://www.ratical.org/ratville/JFK/MLKACT/MapMemphis.html

"Assassination Conspiracy Trial." *Thekingcenter.Org.*

"Findings on MLK Assassination." *Archives.Gov.* The U.S. National Archives and Records
Administration. Web.
https://www.archives.gov/research/jfk/select-committee-report/part-2d.html

Pease, Lisa. "James Earl Ray Didn't Kill Martin Luther King, Said Dexter King."
Realhistoryarchives.Blogspot.Com. Real History Blog, 4 Apr. 1968. Web.
http://realhistoryarchives.blogspot.com/2008/04/james-earl-ray-didnt-kill-martin-luther.html

Sergeant, John and John Edginton. "The Conspiracy to Kill Martin Luther King."

Allen, Nick. "Trusted Martin Luther King Civil Rights Photographer was FBI Informant."
Telegraph.Co.Uk. The Telegraph, 14 Sept. 2010. Web.
http://www.telegraph.co.uk/news/worldnews/northamerica/usa/8002629/Trusted-Martin-Luther-King-
civil-rights-photographer-was-FBI-informant.html

Chapter 18

"Assassination Conspiracy Trial." *Thekingcenter.Org.* (1521, etc.)

Sides, Hampton.

Melanson, Philip H. "The Martin Luther King Assassination." Charlotte: S.P.I. Books, 1994. Google Books. Web.
https://goo.gl/9uMSZ1

"The Transcription of the King Family Press Conference on the MLK Assassination Trial Verdict." 9 Dec. 1999. *Thekingcenter.Org.* The King Center. Web
http://www.thekingcenter.org/sites/default/files/Assassination%20Trial%20-%20Family%20Press%20Conference.pdf

"Intelligence Related Commissions, Other Select or Special Committees and Special Reports." *Intelligence.Senate.Gov.* U.S. Senate Select Committee on Intelligence. Web.
http://www.intelligence.senate.gov/resources/intelligence-related-commissions (See Senate Select Committee to Study Governmental Operations with Respect to Intelligence Activities, 1975-1976 [Church Committee], Book III, pg. 135)

King, Martin Luther, Jr. "Letter From A Birmingham Jail." Birmingham, AL, 16 Apr. 1963. *Kinginstitute.Stanford.Edu.* The King Institute. Web.
https://kinginstitute.stanford.edu/king-papers/documents/letter-birmingham-jail

Harris, Malcolm. "The Psychology of Torture." *Aeon.Co.* Aeon, 7 Oct. 2014. Web.
https://aeon.co/essays/is-it-time-to-stop-doing-any-more-milgram-experiments

"Pentagon Papers: The Secret War." *Cnn.Com.* All Politics. Time, 28 June 1971. Web.
http://www.cnn.com/ALLPOLITICS/1996/analysis/back.time/9606/28/index.shtml

"Pentagon Papers." *U-s-history.Com.* Online Highways. Web.
http://www.u-s-history.com/pages/h1871.html http://study.com/academy/lesson/pentagon-papers-definition-summary.html

Fifield, Anna. "Contractors Reap $138B From Iraq War." *Cnn.Com.* CNN, 19 Mar. 2013. Web.
https://www.cnn.com/2013/03/19/business/iraq-war-contractors/

Young, Angelo. "Cheney's Halliburton Made $39.5 Billion on Iraq War." *Readersupportednews.Org.* Reader Supported News, 20 Mar. 2013. Web.
http://readersupportednews.org/news-section2/308-12/16561-focus-cheneys-halliburton-made-395-billion-on-iraq-war

Cray, Charlie. "General Electric." *Corpwatch.Org.* Corp Watch. Web.
http://www.corpwatch.org/section.php?id=16

Lee, Eloise and Robert Johnson. "The 25 Biggest Defense Companies in America."
Businessinsider.Com. Business Insider, 13 Mar. 2012. Web.
http://www.businessinsider.com/top-25-us-defense-companies-2012-2?op=1

Sullivan, Danny. "How Google Instant's Autocomplete Suggestions Work." *Searchengineland.Com*.
Third Door Media, 6 Apr. 2011. Web.
http://searchengineland.com/how-google-instant-autocomplete-suggestions-work-62592

Chapter 19

Dodson, Howard. "How Slavery Helped Build a World Economy." *News.Nationalgeographic.Com*.
National Geographic News, 3 Feb. 2003. Web.
https://news.nationalgeographic.com/news/2003/01/0131_030203_jubilee2.html

"Historical Context: Was Slavery the Engine of American Economic Growth?" *Gilderlehrman.Org*.
The Gilder Lehrman Institute of American History. Web.
http://www.gilderlehrman.org/history-by-era/slavery-and-anti-slavery/resources/was-slavery-engine-
american-economic-growth

Grandin, Greg. "Capitalism and Slavery." *Thenation.Com*. The Nation, 1 May 2015. Web.
https://www.thenation.com/article/capitalism-and-slavery/

Sinn, Mike P. "Government Spends More on Corporate Welfare Subsidies Than Social Welfare
Programs." *Thinkbynumbers.Org*. Think By Numbers. Web.
https://thinkbynumbers.org/government-spending/corporate-welfare/corporate-vs-social-welfare/

Bivens, Josh and Lawrence Mishel. "Understanding the Historic Divergence Between Productivity and
a Typical Worker's Pay." *Epi.Org*. Economic Policy Institute, 2 Sept. 2015. Web.
http://www.epi.org/publication/understanding-the-historic-divergence-between-productivity-and-a-
typical-workers-pay-why-it-matters-and-why-its-real/

Mishel, Lawrence, Elise Gould and Josh Bivens. "Wage Stagnation in Nine Charts." *Epi.Org*.
Economic Policy Institute, 6 Jan. 2015. Web.
http://www.epi.org/publication/charting-wage-stagnation/

Gilson, Dave. "Overworked America: 12 Charts That Will Make Your Blood Boil." *Motherjones.Com*.
Mother Jones, July/Aug. 2011. Web.
http://www.motherjones.com/politics/2011/06/speedup-americans-working-harder-charts

Futrelle, David. "Is Middle Class Stagnation Really a Myth?" *Business.Time.Com*. Time, 1 Feb. 2013.
Web.
http://business.time.com/2013/02/01/is-middle-class-stagnation-really-a-myth/

Milligan, Susan. "Poverty, Wages Remain Stagnant Despite Economic Recovery." *Usnews.Com*. U.S.
News and World Report, 16 Sept. 2015. Web.

http://www.usnews.com/news/articles/2015/09/16/poverty-wages-remain-stagnant-despite-economic-recovery

Gould, Elise. "The State of American Wages 2017." *Epi.Org*. Economic Policy Institute, 1 Mar. 2018. Web.
https://www.epi.org/publication/the-state-of-american-wages-2017-wages-have-finally-recovered-from-the-blow-of-the-great-recession-but-are-still-growing-too-slowly-and-unequally/

Hungerford, Thomas L. "Corporate Tax Rates and Economic Growth Since 1947." *Epi.Org*. Economic Policy Institute, 4 June 2013. Web.
http://www.epi.org/publication/ib364-corporate-tax-rates-and-economic-growth/

Roach, Brian. "Corporate Power in a Global Economy." *Ase.Tufts.Edu*. Global Development and Environment Institute, Tufts University, 2007. Web.
http://www.ase.tufts.edu/gdae/education_materials/modules/Corporate_Power_in_a_Global_Economy.pdf

Groden, Claire. "Apple and Microsoft Linked to Child Labor in Cobalt Supply Chains." *Fortune.Com*. Fortune, 19, Jan. 2016. Web.
http://fortune.com/2016/01/19/apple-child-labor/

"Democratic Republic of Congo: 'This is What We Die For': Human Rights Abuses in the Democratic Republic of the Congo Power the Global Trade in Cobalt." *Amnesty.Org*. Amnesty International, 19 Jan 2016. Web.
https://www.amnesty.org/en/documents/afr62/3183/2016/en/

Clarke, Joe. "Child Labour on Nestle Farms: Chocolate Giant's Problems Continue." *Theguardian.Com*. The Guardian, 2 Sept. 2015. Web.
https://www.theguardian.com/global-development-professionals-network/2015/sep/02/child-labour-on-nestle-farms-chocolate-giants-problems-continue

Manik, Julfikar and Jim Yardley. "Building Collapse in Bangladesh Leaves Scores Dead." *Nytimes.Com*. The New York Times, 24 Apr. 2013. Web.
http://www.nytimes.com/2013/04/25/world/asia/bangladesh-building-collapse.html?pagewanted=all

O'Toole, James. "GAO: U.S. Corporations Pay Average Effective Tax Rate of 12.6%." *Money.Cnn.Com*. CNN, 1 July 2013. Web.
http://money.cnn.com/2013/07/01/news/economy/corporate-tax-rate/White, James. "Corporate

Income Tax: Effective Tax Rates Can Differ Significantly from the Statutory Rate." *Gao.Gov*. United States Government Accountability Office, May 2013. Web.
http://www.gao.gov/assets/660/654957.pdf

"The Sorry State of Corporate Taxes." *Ctj.Org*. Citizens for Tax Justice. Web.
https://www.ctj.org/the-sorry-state-of-corporate-taxes/

"The 35 Percent Corporate Tax Myth." *Itep.Org.* Institute on Taxation and Economic Policy, 9 Mar. 2017. Web.
https://itep.org/the-35-percent-corporate-tax-myth/

Kurtzleben, Danielle. "Fact Check: Does the U.S. Have the Highest Corporate Tax Rate in the World?" *Npr.Org.* NPR, 7 Aug. 2017. Web.
https://www.npr.org/2017/08/07/541797699/fact-check-does-the-u-s-have-the-highest-corporate-tax-rate-in-the-world

Bentley, Daniel. "The Top 1% Now Owns Half the World's Wealth." *Fortune.Com.* Time Inc., 14 Oct. 2015. Web.
http://fortune.com/2015/10/14/1-percent-global-wealth-credit-suisse/

Stierli, Markus. . . . "Global Wealth Report 2015." *Publications.Credit-suisse.Com.* Credit Suisse AG, Oct. 2015. Web.
https://publications.credit-suisse.com/tasks/render/file/?fileID=F2425415-DCA7-80B8-EAD989AF9341D47E

"Richest 1 Percent Bagged 82 Percent of Wealth Crated Last Year - Poorest Half of Humanity Got Nothing." *Oxfam.Org.* Oxfam International, 22 Jan. 2018. Web.
https://www.oxfam.org/en/pressroom/pressreleases/2018-01-22/richest-1-percent-bagged-82-percent-wealth-created-last-year

Pimentel, Diego, Inigo Aymar and Max Lawson. "Reward Work, Not Wealth." *Oxfam.Org.* Oxfam International, Jan. 2018. Web.
https://www.oxfam.org/en/research/reward-work-not-wealth
https://d1tn3vj7xz9fdh.cloudfront.net/s3fs-public/file_attachments/bp-reward-work-not-wealth-220118-en.pdf

Gebeloff, Robert and Shaila Dewan. "Measuring the Top 1% by Wealth, Not Income." *Economix.Blogs.Nytimes.Com.* The New York Times, 17 Jan. 2012. Web.
https://economix.blogs.nytimes.com/2012/01/17/measuring-the-top-1-by-wealth-not-income/

"Federal Corporate Income Tax Rates, Income Years 1909-2012." *Taxfoundation.Org.* Tax Foundation, 6 July 2012. Web.
https://taxfoundation.org/federal-corporate-income-tax-rates-income-years-1909-2012/

"Individual and Corporate Tax Data." *Smbiz.Com.* A/N Group. Web.
http://www.smbiz.com/sbrl001.html

El-Sibaie, Amir. "2018 Tax Brackets (Updated)." *Files.Taxfoundation.Org.* Tax Foundation, Jan. 2018. Web.
https://files.taxfoundation.org/20180207142513/TaxFoundation-FF567-Updated.pdf

Murray, Jean. "Corporate Tax Rates and What You Owe." *Thebalancesmb.Com.* The Balance Small Business, 5 Feb. 2018. Web.
https://www.thebalancesmb.com/corporate-tax-rates-and-tax-calculation-397647

Boesler, Matthew. "Here's How America's Minimum Wage Stacks Up Against Countries Like India, Russia, Greece, and France." *Businessinsider.Com.* Business Insider, 19 Aug. 2013. Web.
http://www.businessinsider.com/a-look-at-minimum-wages-around-the-world-2013-8

Mattera, Philip. "Subsidizing the Corporate One Percent . . ." *Goodjobsfirst.Org.* Good Jobs First, Feb. 2014. Web.
http://www.goodjobsfirst.org/sites/default/files/docs/pdf/subsidizingthecorporateonepercent.pdf

Bryan, Bob. "It's Here: All the Details of Trump's Massive Tax Plan." *Businessinsider.Com.* Business Insider, 27 Sept. 2017. Web.
http://www.businessinsider.com/trump-tax-plan-details-corporate-rate-individual-brackets-deductions-cuts-2017-9

Gandel, Stephen. "Pfizer's Allergan Deal is an Even Bigger Tax Dodge That It's Claiming." *Fortune.Com.* Time Inc., 24 Nov. 2015. Web.
http://fortune.com/2015/11/24/pfizer-allergan-taxes/

"Top Spenders." *Opensecrets.Org.* The Center for Responsive Politics. Web.
https://www.opensecrets.org/lobby/top.php?indexType=s

Chapter 20

Gopnik, Adam. "The John Birchers' Tea Party." *Newyorker.com.* The New Yorker, 11 Oct. 2013. Web.
https://www.newyorker.com/news/daily-comment/the-john-birchers-tea-party

"John Birch Society Labels South Africa's Mandela a 'Communist Terrorist Thug.'" *Historycommons.Org.* History Commons, 11 Dec. 2009.
http://www.historycommons.org/entity.jsp?entity=clint_eastwood_1

Latson, Jennifer. "How the John Birch Society was Founded." *Time.Com.* Time, 9 Dec. 2014. Web.
http://time.com/3623761/john-birch/

"Rachel Maddow Exposes Fascist John Birch Society." *Youtube.Com.* YouTube. Web.
https://www.youtube.com/watch?v=59M_Or0DWhI

"Fred Koch." *Jbs.Org.* The John Birch Society. Web.
https://www.jbs.org/about-jbs/fred-koch

"'Hidden History' of Koch Brothers Traces Their Childhood and Political Rise." Fresh Air. *Npr.Org.* NPR, 19 Jan. 2016. Web.
http://www.npr.org/2016/01/19/463565987/hidden-history-of-koch-brothers-traces-their-childhood-and-political-rise

"Richest People in the World: Forbes' Top 20 Billionaires of 2018." *Cbsnews.Com.* CBS News. Web.
https://www.cbsnews.com/pictures/richest-people-in-world-forbes/

Mayer, Jane. "Who Sponsored the Hate?" *Newyorker.Com.* The New Yorker, 15 Mar. 2016. Web.
http://www.newyorker.com/news/news-desk/who-sponsored-the-hate

Mayer, Jane. "Covert Operations." *Newyorker.Com.* The New Yorker, 30 Aug. 2010. Web.
http://www.newyorker.com/magazine/2010/08/30/covert-operations

Eilperin, Juliet. "Anatomy of a Washington Dinner: Who Funds the Competitive Enterprise Institute?"
Washingtonpost.Com. The Washington Post, 20 June 2013. Web.
https://www.washingtonpost.com/news/the-fix/wp/2013/06/20/anatomy-of-a-washington-dinner-who-
funds-the-competitive-enterprise-institute/?utm_term=.5c93f3ddf3f5

Young, Chris. "Why are the Kochs Investing in Happiness?" *Slate.Com.* Slate, 25 June 2014. Web.
http://www.slate.com/technology/2018/03/mike-pompeo-doesnt-believe-in-climate-change.html

Allen, Mike and Jim Vandehei. "The Koch Brothers' Secret Bank." *Politico.Com.* Politico, 11 Sept.
2013. Web.
https://www.politico.com/story/2013/09/behind-the-curtain-exclusive-the-koch-brothers-secret-bank-
096669

Choma, Russ. "Koch Industries, Business Groups Lobby Against Donor Disclosure." *Opensecrets.Org.*
The Center for Responsive Politics, 25 Apr. 2013. Web.
https://www.opensecrets.org/news/2013/04/koch-industries-and-business-groups/

"Challenge Accepted." *Kochind.Com.* Koch Industries. Web.
http://www.kochind.com/ (3/16/2018)

"About." *Cei.Org.* Competitive Enterprise Institute. Web.
https://cei.org/about-cei

Eilperin, Juliet. "Anatomy of a Washington Dinner: Who Funds the Competitive Enterprise Institute?"
Washingtonpost.Com. The Washington Post, 20 June 2013. Web.
https://www.washingtonpost.com/news/the-fix/wp/2013/06/20/anatomy-of-a-washington-dinner-who-
funds-the-competitive-enterprise-institute/?utm_term=.5c93f3ddf3f5

"U.S. Constitution - Article 1 Section 8." *U.s.constitution.net.* Usconstitution.net. Web.
https://www.usconstitution.net/xconst_A1Sec8.html

Porter, Robert. "Contract Claims Against the Federal Government: Sovereign Immunity and
Contractual Remedies." *Law.Harvard.Edu.* Harvard Law School, 2 May 2006. Web.
http://www.law.harvard.edu/faculty/hjackson/ContractClaims_22.pdf

Lobato, John and Jeffrey Theodore. "The Scope of Sovereign Immunity." *Law.Harvard.Edu.* Harvard
Law School, 14 May 2006. Web.
http://www.law.harvard.edu/faculty/hjackson/FedSovereign_21.pdf

Jackson, Vicki C. "Suing the Federal Government: Sovereignty, Immunity, and Judicial Independence."
Scholarship.Law.Georgetown.Edu. Georgetown University Law Center, 2003. Web.
https://scholarship.law.georgetown.edu/cgi/viewcontent.cgi?referer=&httpsredir=1&article=1111&cont
ext=facpub

Sisk, Gregory C. "The Continuing Drift of Federal Sovereign Immunity Jurisprudence."
Scholarship.Law.Wm.Edu. William and Mary Law Review, Vol. 50, Issue 2, 2008.
http://scholarship.law.wm.edu/cgi/viewcontent.cgi?article=1060&context=wmlr

"Sovereign Immunity." *Legal-Dictionary.Thefreedictionary.Com.* The Free Dictionary by Farlex. Web.
http://legal-dictionary.thefreedictionary.com/Sovereign+Immunity

Vincent, Carol Hardy, Laura A. Hanson and Carla N. Argueta. "Federal Land Ownership: Overview
and Data." *Fas.Org.* Congressional Research Service, 3 Mar. 2017. Web.
http://fas.org/sgp/crs/misc/R42346.pdf

Timberg, Craig and Barton Gellman. "NSA Paying U.S. Companies for Access to Communications
Networks." *Washingtonpost.Com.* The Washington Post, 29 Aug. 2013. Web.
https://www.washingtonpost.com/world/national-security/nsa-paying-us-companies-for-access-to-
communications-networks/2013/08/29/5641a4b6-10c2-11e3-bdf6-
e4fc677d94a1_story.html?utm_term=.0655380ffb05

Savage, Charlie. "Obama Administration Set to Expand Sharing of Data That N.S.A. Intercepts."
Nytimes.Com. The New York Times, 25 Feb. 2016. Web.
https://www.nytimes.com/2016/02/26/us/politics/obama-administration-set-to-expand-sharing-of-data-
that-nsa-intercepts.html

Balko, Radley. "Surprise! NSA Data Will Soon Routinely be Used for Domestic Policing That has
Nothing to do With Terrorism." *Washingtonpost.Com.* The Washington Post, 10 Mar. 2016. Web.
https://www.washingtonpost.com/news/the-watch/wp/2016/03/10/surprise-nsa-data-will-soon-
routinely-be-used-for-domestic-policing-that-has-nothing-to-do-with-terrorism/

Kayyali, Dia. "How the NSA is Transforming Law Enforcement." *Eff.Org.* Electronic Frontier
Foundation, 20 May 2014. Web.
https://www.eff.org/deeplinks/2014/05/how-nsa-transforming-law-enforcement

Kelly, John. "Cellphone Data Spying: It's Not Just the NSA." *Usatoday.Com.* USA Today. Web.
http://www.usatoday.com/story/news/nation/2013/12/08/cellphone-data-spying-nsa-police/3902809/

Eaton, Joshua. "NSA Data-Sharing Plan Opens Door to Mass Surveillance, Say Rights Groups."
Csmonitor.Com. The Christian Science Monitor, 7 Apr. 2016. Web.
https://www.csmonitor.com/World/Passcode/2016/0407/NSA-data-sharing-plan-opens-door-to-mass-
surveillance-say-rights-groups

"Surveillance Techniques: How Your Data Becomes Our Data." *Nsa.Gov1.Info.* Domestic Surveillance
Directorate. Web.
https://nsa.gov1.info/surveillance/index.html

"Your Data: If You Have Nothing to Hide, You Have Nothing to Fear." *Nsa.Gov1.Info*. Domestic Surveillance Directorate. Web.
https://nsa.gov1.info/data/

Schneier, Bruce. "NSA Surveillance: A Guide to Staying Secure." *Theguardian.com*. The Guardian, 6 Sept. 2013. Web.
https://www.theguardian.com/world/2013/sep/05/nsa-how-to-remain-secure-surveillance

Kelly, John. "Cellphone Data Spying: It's Not Just the NSA." *Usatoday.Com*. USA Today. Web.
http://www.usatoday.com/story/news/nation/2013/12/08/cellphone-data-spying-nsa-police/3902809/

"Dep't of Justice, New Department Policy Concerning Electronic Recording of Statements." *Harvardlawreview.Org*. Harvard Law Review, 10 Mar. 2015. Web.
http://harvardlawreview.org/2015/03/dept-of-justice-new-department-policy-concerning-electronic-recording-of-statements/

McKinley, James C. and Joseph Goldstein. "Confession in 'Baby Hope' Killing was Taped, but the Interrogation was Not."*Nytimes.Com*. The New York Times, 23 Oct. 2013. Web.
http://www.nytimes.com/2013/10/24/nyregion/police-didnt-tape-baby-hope-questioning.html?_r=0

"FBI to Record all Suspect Interviews in Major policy Shift." *Bbc.Com*. BBC, 22 May 2014. Web.
http://www.bbc.com/news/world-us-canada-27527125

"FBI Memo." *Nytimes.Com*. The New York Times.
http://www.nytimes.com/packages/pdf/national/20070402_FBI_Memo.pdf

Bump, Phillip. "Do You Know the Difference Between a Communist and a Socialist?" *Independent.Co.Uk*. Independent, 25 Oct. 2015. Web.
http://www.independent.co.uk/news/world/americas/do-you-know-the-difference-between-a-communist-and-a-socialist-a6708086.html

Irons, John and Isaac Shapiro. "Regulation, Employment, and the Economy." *Epi.Org*. Economic Policy Institute, 12 Apr. 2011. Web.
http://www.epi.org/publication/regulation_employment_and_the_economy_fears_of_job_loss_are_overblown/

"We Fight For Freedom." *Americansforprosperity.Org*. Americans for Prosperity. Web.
https://americansforprosperity.org/

"Scientific Consensus: Earth's Climate is Warming." *Climate.Nasa.Gov*. NASA. Web.
http://climate.nasa.gov/scientific-consensus/ https://climate.nasa.gov/causes/

"Causes of Climate Change." *Epa.Gov*. EPA. Web.
https://19january2017snapshot.epa.gov/climate-change-science/causes-climate-change_.html
https://www.epa.gov/sites/production/files/signpost/cc.html

"How do we Know That Humans are the Major Cause of Global Warming?" *Ucsusa.Org.* Union of Concerned Scientists, 1 Aug. 2017. Web.
https://www.ucsusa.org/global-warming/science-and-impacts/science/human-contribution-to-gw-faq.html#.WrD_NcPwbIU

"Goal 13: Take Urgent Action to Combat Climate Change and its Impacts." *Un.Org.* United Nations. Web.
http://www.un.org/sustainabledevelopment/climate-change-2/

"Known and Probable Human Carcinogens." *Cancer.Org.* American Cancer Society, 3 Nov. 2016. Web.
https://www.cancer.org/cancer/cancer-causes/general-info/known-and-probable-human-carcinogens.html

Goldenberg, Suzanne. "Leak Exposes how Heartland Institute Works to Undermine Climate Science." *Theguardian.Com.* The Guardian, 14 Feb. 2012. Web.
https://www.theguardian.com/environment/2012/feb/15/leak-exposes-heartland-institute-climate

Robertson, Lori. "AFP Distorts Begich's Carbon Tax Stance." *Factcheck.Org.* Factcheck.Org, 28 Feb. 2014. Web.
http://www.factcheck.org/2014/02/afp-distorts-begichs-carbon-tax-stance/

"About Cato." *Cato.Org.* Cato Institute. Web.
https://www.cato.org/about

"About Heritage." *Heritage.Org.* The Heritage Foundation. Web.
http://www.heritage.org/about

"Our Mission." *Jbs.Org.* The John Birch Society. Web.
https://www.jbs.org/about-jbs

Beckel, Michael. "Koch-backed Nonprofit Spent Record Cash in 2012." *Publicintegrity.Org.* The Center for Public Integrity, 14 Nov. 2013. Web.
https://www.publicintegrity.org/2013/11/14/13712/koch-backed-nonprofit-spent-record-cash-2012

Mattera, Philip. "Koch Industries: Corporate Rap Sheet." *Corp-research.Org.* Corporate Research Project. Web.
https://www.corp-research.org/koch_industries

Loder, Asjylyn and David Evans. "Koch Brothers Flout Law Getting Richer With Iran Sales." *Bloomberg.com.* Bloomberg Markets, 3 Oct. 2011. Web.
http://www.bloomberg.com/news/articles/2011-10-02/koch-brothers-flout-law-getting-richer-with-secret-iran-sales

Schor, Elana. "Koch Leaves Federal Cancer Panel as Groups Urge Ethics Probe." *Archive.Nytimes.Com.* The New York Times, 27 Oct. 2010.

http://www.nytimes.com/gwire/2010/10/27/27greenwire-koch-leaves-federal-cancer-panel-as-groups-urg-61710.html

"Violation Tracker." *Goodjobsfirst.org*. Good Jobs First. Web.
https://www.goodjobsfirst.org/violation-tracker goo.gl/yhg2kJ

Thomsen, Jacqueline. "Charles Koch Donated $500K to Ryan Days After GOP Tax Plan Passed."
Thehill.Com. The Hill, 21 Jan. 2018. Web.
http://thehill.com/homenews/campaign/370037-charles-koch-donated-500k-to-ryan-days-after-gop-tax-plan-passed

"Koch Industries, Money to Congressional Candidates: 2018 Cycle." *Opensecrets.Org*. The Center for
Responsive Politics, 2018. Web.
https://www.opensecrets.org/orgs/toprecips.php?id=D000000186&cycle=2018

Dwyer, Jim. "What Happened to Jane Mayer When She Wrote About the Koch Brothers?"
Nytimes.Com. The New York Times, 26 Jan. 2016. Web.
https://www.nytimes.com/2016/01/27/nyregion/what-happened-to-jane-mayer-when-she-wrote-about-the-koch-brothers.html?_r=0

Bloom, Deborah and Jareen Imam. "New York Man Dies After Chokehold by Police." *Cnn.Com*. CNN,
8 Dec. 2014. Web.
http://www.cnn.com/2014/07/20/justice/ny-chokehold-death/

Baker, Al, David Goodman and Benjamin Mueller. "Beyond the Chokehold: The Path to Eric Garner's
Death." *Nytimes.Com*. The New York Times, 13 June 2015. Web.
https://www.nytimes.com/2015/06/14/nyregion/eric-garner-police-chokehold-staten-island.html

Weaver, Teri. "Millions up in Smoke: NY has Nation's Highest Cigarette Tax; Why do So Few Pay it?"
Syracuse.Com. The Post-Standard, 13 Dec. 2015. Web.
http://www.syracuse.com/state/index.ssf/2015/12/ny_losing_big_with_nations_highest_cigarette_tax.html

Dunbar, John. "The 'Citizens United' Decision and Why it Matters." *Publicintegrity.Org*. The Center
For Public Integrity, 18 Oct. 2012. Web.
https://www.publicintegrity.org/2012/10/18/11527/citizens-united-decision-and-why-it-matters

Stohr, Greg. "Bloomberg Poll: Americans Want Supreme Court to Turn Off Political Spending Spigot."
Bloomberg.Com. Bloomberg Politics, 28 Sept. 2015. Web.
https://www.bloomberg.com/politics/articles/2015-09-28/bloomberg-poll-americans-want-supreme-court-to-turn-off-political-spending-spigot

Chapter 21

"Who is Helped or Hurt by the Citizens United Decision?" *Washingtonpost.Com*. The Washington Post,
24 Jan. 2010. Web.

http://www.washingtonpost.com/wp-dyn/content/article/2010/01/22/AR2010012203874.html

Gongloff, Mark. "JPMorgan Chase Spent $8 Million on Lobbying Last Year, More Than Any Other Bank." *Huffingtonpost.Com.* HuffPost, 31 May 2013.
https://www.huffingtonpost.com/2013/05/31/jpmorgan-chase-lobbying_n_3366658.html

Culver, John C. and John Hyde. "American Dreamer." New York: W.W. Norton & Company Inc., 2001. Print.

Latson, Jennifer. "How the John Birch Society was Founded." *Time.Com.* Time, 9 Dec. 2014. Web.
http://time.com/3623761/john-birch/

Avlon, John. "A Beloved Icon in Death, in Life Kennedy was Hated by Many." *Telegraph.Co.Uk.* The Telegraph, 23 Nov. 2013. Web.
http://www.telegraph.co.uk/news/worldnews/us-politics/10469889/A-beloved-icon-in-death-in-life-Kennedy-was-hated-by-many.html

Ye Hee Lee, Michelle. "Frank Marshall Davis: Obama's 'Communist' Mentor?'" *Washingtonpost.Com.* The Washington Post, 23 Mar. 2015. Web.
http://www.telegraph.co.uk/news/worldnews/us-politics/10469889/A-beloved-icon-in-death-in-life-Kennedy-was-hated-by-many.html

Mitter, Rana. "Forgotten Ally? China's Unsung Role in World War II." *Cnn.Com.* CNN, 31 Aug. 2015. Web.
http://www.cnn.com/2015/08/31/opinions/china-wwii-forgotten-ally-rana-mitter/

"Nuclear Weapons Timeline." *Icanw.Org.* International Campaign to Abolish Nuclear Weapons. Web.
http://www.icanw.org/the-facts/the-nuclear-age/

McCauley, David. "Almost 70 Years After the Bombings of Hiroshima and Nagasaki." *Afsc.Org.* American Friends Service Committee, 16 July 2014. Web.
https://www.afsc.org/story/almost-70-years-after-bombings-hiroshima-and-nagasaki

Akin, Jimmy. "Two Unsuccessful Arguments for Bombing Hiroshima and Nagasaki." *Ncregister.Com.* National Catholic Register, 8 Aug. 2016. Web.
http://www.ncregister.com/blog/jimmy-akin/two-unsuccessful-arguments-for-bombing-hiroshima-and-nagasaki

Southard, Susan. "What U.S. Citizens Weren't Told About the Atomic Bombing of Japan." *Latimes.Com.* Los Angeles Times, 7 Aug. 2015. Web.
http://www.latimes.com/opinion/op-ed/la-oe-0809-southard-atomic-bomb-survivors-20150806-story.html

Hall, Michelle. "By the Numbers: World War II's Atomic Bombs." *Cnn.Com.* CNN, 6 Aug. 2013. Web.
https://www.cnn.com/2013/08/06/world/asia/btn-atomic-bombs/

"Nuclear Arsenals." *Icanw.Org.* International Campaign to Abolish Nuclear Weapons. Web.

http://www.icanw.org/the-facts/nuclear-arsenals/

Oliver Stone. "Oliver Stone's Untold History of the United States." *Netflix.Com.* Netflix, 2013. Web.

"House Committee on Un-American Activities." *Encyclopedia.com.* Dictionary of American History, 22 Mar. 2018. Web.
https://www.encyclopedia.com/history/united-states-and-canada/us-history/house-un-american-activities-committee

Anderson, Jack and Dale Van Atta. "Apparently the FBI did not Love Lucy." *Washingtonpost.Com.* The Washington Post, 7 Dec. 1989. Web.
https://www.washingtonpost.com/archive/business/1989/12/07/apparently-the-fbi-did-not-love-lucy/ca6ccf7b-269b-4992-abb8-26afef7bae28/?utm_term=.e7c90c8ff180

Devinatz, Victor G. "Communist Party of the United States of America." *Britannica.Com.* Encyclopaedia Britannica. Web.
https://www.britannica.com/topic/Communist-Party-of-the-United-States-of-America

Lewis, Aidan. "The Curious Survival of the US Communist Party." *Bbc.Com.* BBC, 1 May 2014. Web.
http://www.bbc.com/news/magazine-26126325

King, Martin Luther. "Keep Moving From This Mountain." Address at Spelman College, Atlanta, Georgia, 10 Apr. 1960. *Kinginstitute.Stanford.Edu.* The King Institute. Web.
https://kinginstitute.stanford.edu/king-papers/documents/keep-moving-mountain-address-spelman-college-10-april-1960

St. Clair, Jeffrey. "The Making of Halliburton." *Counterpunch.Org.* CounterPunch, 14 July 2005. Web.
http://www.counterpunch.org/2005/07/14/the-making-of-halliburton/

Simkin, John. "Clinton Murchison Sr." *Spartacus-educational.Com.* Spartacus Educational. Web.
http://spartacus-educational.com/JFKmurchison.htm

Pepper, William. "The Plot to Kill King." New York: Skyhorse Publishing, 2016. Google Books. Web.
https://goo.gl/1ktEWi

Eilperin, Juliet. "Anatomy of a Washington Dinner: Who Funds the Competitive Enterprise Institute?" *Washingtonpost.Com.* The Washington Post, 20 June 2013. Web.
https://www.washingtonpost.com/news/the-fix/wp/2013/06/20/anatomy-of-a-washington-dinner-who-funds-the-competitive-enterprise-institute/?utm_term=.5c93f3ddf3f5

Rosier, Paul C. "The Long War on Environmentalism." *Medium.Com.* Lepage Center for History in the Public Interest at Villanova University, 13 Oct. 2017. Web.
https://medium.com/hindsights/the-long-war-on-environmentalism-376f2f0d16ca

"Known and Probable Human Carcinogens." *Cancer.Org.* American Cancer Society, 3 Nov. 2016. Web.

https://www.cancer.org/cancer/cancer-causes/general-info/known-and-probable-human-carcinogens.html

Kolbert, Elizabeth. "The E.P.A.'s Dangerous Anti-Regulatory Policies." *Newyorker.Com.* The New Yorker, 30 June 2017. Web.
https://www.newyorker.com/news/daily-comment/the-epas-dangerous-anti-regulatory-policies

DiLorenzo, Thomas J. "Why Socialism Causes Pollution." *Fee.Org.* Foundation for Economic Education, 1 Mar. 1992. Web.
https://fee.org/articles/why-socialism-causes-pollution/

"Scientific Consensus: Earth's Climate is Warming." *Climate.Nasa.Gov.* NASA. Web.
http://climate.nasa.gov/scientific-consensus/ https://climate.nasa.gov/causes/

"Causes of Climate Change." *Epa.Gov.* EPA. Web.
https://19january2017snapshot.epa.gov/climate-change-science/causes-climate-change .html
https://www.epa.gov/sites/production/files/signpost/cc.html

"How do we Know That Humans are the Major Cause of Global Warming?" *Ucsusa.Org.* Union of Concerned Scientists, 1 Aug. 2017. Web.
https://www.ucsusa.org/global-warming/science-and-impacts/science/human-contribution-to-gw-faq.html#.WrD_NcPwbIU

"Goal 13: Take Urgent Action to Combat Climate Change and its Impacts." *Un.Org.* United Nations. Web.
http://www.un.org/sustainabledevelopment/climate-change-2/

"Short Answers to Hard Questions About Climate Change." *Nytimes.Com.* The New York Times, 6 July 2017. Web.
https://www.nytimes.com/interactive/2015/11/28/science/what-is-climate-change.html

Oreskes, Naomi. "The Scientific Consensus on Climate Change." *Science.Sciencemag.Org.* Science, 3 Dec. 2004: 1686. Web.
http://science.sciencemag.org/content/306/5702/1686.full

Follett, Andrew. "5 Moneyed Environmentalists who Profit off Global Warming." *Climatechangedispatch.Com.* Daily Caller, 8 Feb. 2016. Web.
http://climatechangedispatch.com/5-moneyed-environmentalists-who-profit-off-global-warming/

"Not Just the Koch Brothers: New Study Reveals Funders Behind Climate Change Denial Effort." *Phys.Org.* Phys.Org, 20 Dec. 2013. Web.
https://phys.org/news/2013-12-koch-brothers-reveals-funders-climate.html

"Bill O'Reilly: Universal Healthcare is Communist." *Youtube.Com.* Secular Talk, 23 Oct. 2013. Web.
https://www.youtube.com/watch?v=hhyP7u1v4tE

Mahadea, Nikhil. "Does Minimum Wage Lead to Communism?" *Intelligentcitizen.Ca.* Intelligent Citizen, 8 Aug. 2017. Web. http://intelligentcitizen.ca/minimum-wage-the-tool-of-a-communist-government/

Dorn, James A. "Minimum Wage Socialism." *Cato.Org.* Cato Institute, 4 July 2006. Web. https://www.cato.org/publications/commentary/minimum-wage-socialism

Irons, John and Isaac Shapiro. "Regulation, Employment, and the Economy." *Epi.Org.* Economic Policy Institute, 12 Apr. 2011. Web. http://www.epi.org/publication/regulation_employment_and_the_economy_fears_of_job_loss_are_ove rblown/

Kaufman, Alexander C. "Mike Pompeo Would be the First Secretary of State to Deny That Climate Change is Real." *Slate.Com.* Slate, 13 Mar. 2018. Web. https://slate.com/technology/2018/03/mike-pompeo-doesnt-believe-in-climate-change.html

Mayer, Jane. "Who Sponsored the Hate?" *Newyorker.Com.* The New Yorker, 15 Mar. 2016. Web. http://www.newyorker.com/news/news-desk/who-sponsored-the-hate

Kotch, Alex. "The Koch Brothers' Most Loyal Servants are Serving in Donald Trump's White House." *Salon.Com.* Alternet, 11 Jan. 2017. Web. http://www.salon.com/2017/01/11/koch-allies-in-the-white-house_partner/

Vogel, Kenneth P. and Eliana Johnson. "Trump's Koch Administration." *Politico.Com.* Politico, 28 Nov. 2016. Web. http://www.politico.com/story/2016/11/trump-koch-brothers-231863

Gilpin, Lyndsey. "Trump's Cabinet Choices Reflect Deep Koch Influence." *Hcn.Org.* High Country News, 15 Dec. 2016. http://www.hcn.org/articles/donald-trumps-cabinet-choices-reflect-koch-influence

"Aftermath: Sixteen Writers on Trump's America." *Newyorker.Com.* The New Yorker, 21 Nov. 2016. Web. http://www.newyorker.com/magazine/2016/11/21/aftermath-sixteen-writers-on-trumps-america

Bourne, Joel K. "In The Arctic's Cold Rush, There are no Easy Profits," *Nationalgeographic.Com.* National Geographic, Mar. 2016. Web. http://www.nationalgeographic.com/magazine/2016/03/new-arctic-thawing-rapidly-circle-work-oil/

DiChristopher, Tom and John W. Schoen. "Trump War on 'Job-Destroying' Regulations Could Kill a lot of High-Paying Jobs." *Cnbc.Com.* CNBC, 8 Dec. 2016. Web. https://www.cnbc.com/2016/12/08/pruitt-epa-trump-may-kill-jobs-fighting-job-destroying-regulations.html

"A Timeline of Heritage Successes." *Heritage.Org.* The Heritage Foundation. Web. https://www.heritage.org/about-heritage/impact

Chapter 22

Hargreaves, Steve. "Making it Into the Middle Class." *Economy.Money.Cnn.Com.* CNN, 13 Nov. 2013. Web.
http://economy.money.cnn.com/2013/11/13/making-it-into-the-middle-class/

Vincent, Carol Hardy, Laura A. Hanson and Carla N. Argueta. "Federal Land Ownership: Overview and Data." *Fas.Org.* Congressional Research Service, 3 Mar. 2017. Web.
http://fas.org/sgp/crs/misc/R42346.pdf

Chapter 23

Smith, Noah. "Big Companies are Getting a Chokehold on the Economy." *Bloomberg.Com.* Bloomberg, 22 Feb. 2018. Web.
https://www.bloomberg.com/view/articles/2018-02-22/big-companies-gaining-monopoly-power-pose-risk-to-u-s-economy

Roach, Brian. "Corporate Power in a Global Economy." *Ase.Tufts.Edu.* Global Development and Environment Institute, Tufts University, 2007. Web.
http://www.ase.tufts.edu/gdae/education_materials/modules/Corporate_Power_in_a_Global_Economy.pdf

Francis, Jennifer. "Market Power in Economics: Definition, Sources, & Examples." *Study.Com.* Study.com. Web.
https://study.com/academy/lesson/market-power-in-economics-definition-sources-examples.html

Thoma, Mark. "What's so Bad About Monopoly Power?" *Cbsnews.Com.* CBS, 18 Sept. 2014. Web.
http://www.cbsnews.com/news/whats-so-bad-about-monopoly-power/

Wu, Tim. "The Oligopoly Problem." *Newyorker.Com.* The New Yorker, 15 Apr. 2013. Web.
http://www.newyorker.com/tech/elements/the-oligopoly-problem

Mattera, Philip. "Subsidizing the Corporate One Percent . . ." *Goodjobsfirst.Org.* Good Jobs First, Feb. 2014. Web.
http://www.goodjobsfirst.org/sites/default/files/docs/pdf/subsidizingthecorporateonepercent.pdf

"Diversification Using Mergers and Acquisitions - Reasons for Following Acquisition Strategies." *Openlearningworld.Com.* OpenLearningWorld. com. Web.
http://www.openlearningworld.com/books/Corporate%20Strategies/Diversification%20Using%20Mergers%20and%20Acquisitions/Reasons%20for%20following%20Acquisition%20Strategies.html

Vollrath, Dietrich. "There's no Limit to Google's Market Power." *Nytimes.Com.* The New York Times, 28 Apr. 2016. Web.

http://www.nytimes.com/roomfordebate/2016/04/28/is-google-a-harmful-monopoly/theres-no-limit-to-googles-market-power

Harrison, J.D. "The Decline of American Entrepreneurship - in Five Charts." *Washingtonpost.Com.* The Washington Post, 12 Feb. 2015. Web.
https://www.washingtonpost.com/news/on-small-business/wp/2015/02/12/the-decline-of-american-entrepreneurship-in-five-charts/?utm_term=.f3d994e030b8

"Too Much of a Good Thing." *Economist.Com.* The Economist, 26 Mar. 2016. Web.
http://www.economist.com/news/briefing/21695385-profits-are-too-high-america-needs-giant-dose-competition-too-much-good-thing

Cassidy, John. "Why Jean Tirole Won the Economics Nobel." *Newyorker.Com.* The New Yorker, 13 Oct. 2014. Web.
https://www.newyorker.com/news/john-cassidy/worthy-economics-nobel-jean-tirole

"Top Spenders." *Opensecrets.Org.* The Center for Responsive Politics. Web.
https://www.opensecrets.org/lobby/top.php?indexType=s

"U.S. -Egypt Business Council Member Companies." *Usegyptcouncil.Org.* U.S. -Egypt Business Council. Web.
http://www.usegyptcouncil.org/member-companies/ https://www.usegyptcouncil.org/about/
https://www.uschamber.com/international/middle-east-and-turkey/us-egypt-business-council

Fang, Lee. "Revealed: More Corporate Donations to the U.S. Chamber's Partisan Attack Fund." *Thinkprogress.Org.* Think Progress, 22 Oct. 2010. Web.
https://thinkprogress.org/revealed-more-corporate-donations-to-the-u-s-chambers-partisan-attack-fund-44f605df54aa/

"Membership." *Uschamber.Com.* U.S. Chamber of Commerce. Web.
https://www.uschamber.com/membership-0

"Koch Industries: Annual Lobbying by Koch Industries." *Opensecrets.Org.* The Center for Responsive Politics. Web.
https://www.opensecrets.org/lobby/clientsum.php?id=d000000186

Allen, Mike and Jim Vandehei. "The Koch Brothers' Secret Bank." *Politico.Com.* Politico, 11 Sept. 2013. Web.
https://www.politico.com/story/2013/09/behind-the-curtain-exclusive-the-koch-brothers-secret-bank-096669

Leonard, Christopher. "A Look at how Koch Does Business." *Chicagotribune.Com.* Chicago Tribune, 5 Jul. 2017. Web.
http://www.chicagotribune.com/business/ct-koch-industries-georgia-pacific-20170703-story.html

Saperstein, Tess. "Medicated Monopolies." *Harvardpolitics.Com.* Harvard Political Review, 10 Dec. 2015. Web.

http://harvardpolitics.com/covers/medicated-monopolies/

Engelberg, Alfred. "How Government Policy Promotes High Drug Prices." *Healthaffairs.Org.* Health Affairs, 29 Oct. 2015. Web.
https://www.healthaffairs.org/do/10.1377/hblog20151029.051488/full/

Zhou, Wen. "The Patent Landscape of Genetically Modified Organisms." *Sitn.Hms.Harvard.Edu.* Science in the News, 10 Aug. 2015.
http://sitn.hms.harvard.edu/flash/2015/the-patent-landscape-of-genetically-modified-organisms/

Mitchell, Dan. "Why Monsanto Always Wins." *Fortune.Com.* Fortune, 26 June 2014. Web.
http://fortune.com/2014/06/26/monsanto-gmo-crops/

Lincoln, Abraham. "House Divided Speech." Republican State Convention. Springfield, Illinois, 16 June 1858. *Abrahamlincolnonline.Org.* Abraham Lincoln Online. Web.
http://www.abrahamlincolnonline.org/lincoln/speeches/house.htm

Mattera, Philip. "Koch Industries: Corporate Rap Sheet." *Corp-research.Org.* Corporate Research Project. Web.
https://www.corp-research.org/koch_industries

Kilman, Scott. "Cargill Agrees to Pay $24 Million to Settle Civil Price-Fixing Suit." *Wsj.Com.* The Wall Street Journal, 11 Mar. 2004. Web.
https://www.wsj.com/articles/SB107897397133352287

Sullivan, Casey. "Judge Orders Dow Chemical to pay $1.2 Billion in Price-Fixing Case." *Reuters.Com.* Reuters, 15 May 2013. Web.
http://www.reuters.com/article/us-dowchemical-urethane-judgment-idUSBRE94F03R20130516

Dewey, Caitlin. "The Alleged Conspiracy to Fix the Price of Chicken Meat, Explained." *Washingtonpost.Com.* The Washington Post, 1 Feb. 2018. Web.
https://www.washingtonpost.com/news/wonk/wp/2018/02/01/the-alleged-conspiracy-to-fix-the-price-of-chicken-meat-explained/?utm_term=.4fb1a7e60013

"Concentration in Agriculture." *Gao.Gov.* United States Government Accountability Office, 30 June 2009. Web.
http://www.gao.gov/new.items/d09746r.pdf

Daniels, Jeff. "Global Food Prices Around Two-Year High in June as Meat, Dairy and Wheat Climb." *Cnbc.Com.* CNBC, 6 July 2017. Web.
https://www.cnbc.com/2017/07/06/global-food-prices-set-two-year-high-in-june-as-meat-dairy-wheat-climb.html

"What We Do." *Ftc.Gov.* Federal Trade Commission. Web.
https://www.ftc.gov/about-ftc/what-we-do

"The Antitrust Laws." *Ftc.Gov.* Federal Trade Commission. Web.

https://www.ftc.gov/tips-advice/competition-guidance/guide-antitrust-laws/antitrust-laws

"Price Fixing." *Ftc.Gov.* Federal Trade Commission. Web.
https://www.ftc.gov/tips-advice/competition-guidance/guide-antitrust-laws/dealings-competitors/price-fixing

Hayes, Chris. "Transcript: The Breakdown: Are Antitrust Laws a Thing of the Past?" *Thenation.Com.* The Nation, 1 Apr. 2011. Web.
https://www.thenation.com/article/transcript-breakdown-are-antitrust-laws-thing-past/

Newman, Nathan. "15 Years of FTC Failure to Factor Privacy Into Merger Reviews." *Huffingtonpost.Com.* HuffPost, 19 Mar. 2015. Web.
http://www.huffingtonpost.com/nathan-newman/15-years-of-ftc-failure-t_b_6901670.html

Fung, Brian. "A Top Privacy Advocate is Leaving the Federal Trade Commission." *Washingtonpost.Com.* The Washington Post, 22 Mar. 2016. Web.
https://www.washingtonpost.com/news/the-switch/wp/2016/03/22/a-top-privacy-advocate-is-leaving-the-federal-trade-commission/?utm_term=.aa4dc713eaf8

Scola, Nancy. "Exposing ALEC: How Conservative-Backed State Laws are all Connected." *Theatlantic.Com.* The Atlantic, 14 Apr. 2012. Web.
https://www.theatlantic.com/politics/archive/2012/04/exposing-alec-how-conservative-backed-state-laws-are-all-connected/255869/

Graves, Lisa. "ALEC Exposed: The Koch Connection." *Thenation.Com.* The Nation, 12 July 2011. Web.
https://www.thenation.com/article/alec-exposed-koch-connection/

Sloan, Bob. "Alec's Denial of Federal Influence in State Government & Exposing Council for National Policy." *Dailykos.Com.* Daily Kos, 31 May 2011. Web.
https://www.dailykos.com/stories/2011/5/31/979749/-

Ambinder, Marc J. "Inside the Council for National Policy." *Abcnews.Go.Com.* ABC News. Web.
http://abcnews.go.com/Politics/story?id=121170&page=1

"Board of Directors: Linda J. Fischer." *Covanta.Com.* Covanta Holding Corporation. Web.
https://www.covanta.com/About-Covanta/Leadership/Linda-J-Fisher

"Fischer, Linda J. Biography." *2001-2009.State.Gov.* U.S. Department of State. Web.
https://2001-2009.state.gov/g/oes/rls/13005.htm

George Washington University School of Public Health and Health Services. "Conflict-of-interest restrictions needed to ensure strong FDA review." *Sciencedaily.Com.* ScienceDaily, 6 June 2013.
https://www.sciencedaily.com/releases/2013/06/130606154706.htm

Heath, David and Ronnie Greene. "EPA Contaminated by Conflict of Interest." *Pbs.Org.* The Center for Public Integrity, 13 Feb. 2013. Web.

http://www.pbs.org/newshour/spc/multimedia/epa-corporate/

Clowers, Nicole A. "Securities and Exchange Commission: Existing Post-Employment Controls Could be Further Strengthened." *Gao.Gov.* U.S. Government Accountability Office, 12 July 2011. Web. http://www.gao.gov/Products/GAO-11-654

The United States Attorney's Office: Eastern District of Texas. "Former SEC Senior Associate Chief Settles Conflict of Interest Allegations." *Justice.Gov.* United States Department of Justice, 22 Feb. 2016. Web. https://www.justice.gov/usao-edtx/pr/former-sec-senior-associate-chief-settles-conflict-interest-allegations

Allison, Bill. "USDA Nominee Perdue is Cutting Business Ties but Keeping Real Estate." *Bloomberg.Com.* Bloomberg Politics, 12 Mar. 2017. Web. https://www.bloomberg.com/news/articles/2017-03-12/usda-pick-perdue-cutting-business-ties-but-keeping-real-estate

Celarier, Michelle. "Trump Adviser Carl Icahn is a Blinding Supernova of Conflicts of Interest." *Nymag.Com.* New York Magazine, 5 Jan. 2017. http://nymag.com/daily/intelligencer/2017/01/icahn-conflicts-of-interest-trump-white-house.html

Venook, Jeremy. "The Trump Administration's Conflicts of Interest: A Crib Sheet." *TheAtlantic.Com.* The Atlantic, 18 Jan. 2017. Web. https://www.theatlantic.com/business/archive/2017/01/trumps-appointees-conflicts-of-interest-a-crib-sheet/512711/

ABC News. "Nelson Mandela's Most Inspirational Quotes." *Abcnews.Go.Com.* ABC News, 5 Dec. 2013. Web. http://abcnews.go.com/International/nelson-mandelas-inspirational-quotes/story?id=8879848

Telzer, Eva H., **Kathryn L. Humphreys, Mor Shapiro**, and **Nim Tottenham.** "Amygdala Sensitivity to Race Is Not Present in Childhood but Emerges over Adolescence." *Mitpressjournals.Org.* Journal of Cognitive Neuroscience 2013 25:2, 234-244. Web. https://www.mitpressjournals.org/doi/full/10.1162/jocn_a_00311

Woollaston, Victoria. "Mixed-Race Relationships are Making us Taller and Smarter: Children Born to Genetically Diverse Parents are More Intelligent Than Their Ancestors." *Dailymail.Co.Uk.* Daily Mail, 1 July 2015. Web. http://www.dailymail.co.uk/sciencetech/article-3146070/Mixed-race-relationships-making-taller-smarter-Children-born-genetically-diverse-parents-intelligent-ancestors.html

Mishel, Lawrence, Elise Gould and Josh Bivens. "Wage Stagnation in Nine Charts." *Epi.Org.* Economic Policy Institute, 6 Jan. 2015. Web. http://www.epi.org/publication/charting-wage-stagnation/

Norris, Floyd. "Corporate Profits Grow and Wages Slide." *Nytimes.Com.* The New York Times, 4 Apr. 2014. Web.

http://www.nytimes.com/2014/04/05/business/economy/corporate-profits-grow-ever-larger-as-slice-of-economy-as-wages-slide.html

Stahl, Jeremy. "Here are All the Racist Comments That Got Donald Trump Fired From NBC." *Slate.Com.* Slate, 29 June 2015. Web.
http://www.slate.com/blogs/the_slatest/2015/06/29/donald_trump_fired_from_nbc_celebrity_apprentice_star_and_republican_presidential.html

Paris, Valerie. "Why do Americans Spend so Much on Pharmaceuticals?" *Pbs.Org.* PBS, 7 Feb. 2014. Web.
http://www.pbs.org/newshour/updates/americans-spend-much-pharmaceuticals/

Warner, Jennifer. "U.S. Leads the World in Illegal Drug Use." *Cbsnews.Com.* CBS, 1 July 2008. Web.
http://www.cbsnews.com/news/us-leads-the-world-in-illegal-drug-use/

"Rape Rate." *Knoema.Com.* Knoema. Web.
https://knoema.com/atlas/ranks/Rape-rate

"Mexico and United States Compared: Crime Stats." *Nationmaster.Com.* Nation Master. Web.
http://www.nationmaster.com/country-info/compare/Mexico/United-States/Crime

Carroll, Lauren. "Fact-Checking Trump's Claim That Thousands in New Jersey Cheered When World Trade Center Tumbled." *Politifact.Com.* Politifact, 22 Nov. 2015. Web.
http://www.politifact.com/truth-o-meter/statements/2015/nov/22/donald-trump/fact-checking-trumps-claim-thousands-new-jersey-ch/

Costa, Robert and Ed O'Keefe. "House Majority Whip Scalise Confirms he Spoke to White Supremacists in 2002." *Washingtonpost.Com.* The Washington Post, 29 Dec. 2014. Web.
https://www.washingtonpost.com/politics/house-majority-whip-scalise-confirms-he-spoke-to-white-nationalists-in-2002/2014/12/29/7f80dc14-8fa3-11e4-a900-9960214d4cd7_story.html

Badash, David. "Meet the Nine Republicans Still in Congress Who Voted Against Martin Luther King Day." *Thenewcivilrightsmovement.Com.* New Civil Rights Movement, 19 Jan. 2015. Web.
http://www.thenewcivilrightsmovement.com/davidbadash/meet_the_nine_republicans_still_in_congress_who_voted_against_martin_luther_king_day

Kamisar, Ben. "Lawmakers Reflect on MLK Day 'No' Votes." *Thehill.Com.* The Hill, 18 Jan. 2015. Web.
http://thehill.com/homenews/229844-lawmakers-reflect-on-no-votes-on-mlk-day

Sack, Kevin. "Dr. King's Son Says Family Believes Ray is Innocent." *Nytimes.Com.* The New York Times, 28 Mar. 1997. Web.
https://www.nytimes.com/1997/03/28/us/dr-king-s-son-says-family-believes-ray-is-innocent.html

"The Transcription of the King Family Press Conference on the MLK Assassination Trial Verdict." 9 Dec. 1999. *Thekingcenter.Org.* The King Center. Web
http://www.thekingcenter.org/sites/default/files/Assassination%20Trial%20-%20Family%20Press%20Conference.pdf

"Assassination Conspiracy Trial." *Thekingcenter.Org.* The King Center. Web.
http://www.thekingcenter.org/assassination-conspiracy-trial (1483, 1484, 1486)

King, Martin Luther. "Strength to Love." 11 Aug. 1963. *Thekingcenter.Org.* The King Center. Web.
http://www.thekingcenter.org/archive/document/strength-love (35)

King, Martin Luther. "Draft of Chapter II: 'Transformed Nonconformist.'" *Kinginstitute.Stanford.Edu.*
The King Institute. Web.
https://kinginstitute.stanford.edu/king-papers/documents/draft-chapter-ii-transformed-nonconformist

"MLK Quote of the Week: Faith is Taking the First Step . . ." *Thekingcenter.Org.* The King Center, 21
Feb. 2013. Web.
http://www.thekingcenter.org/blog/mlk-quote-week-faith-taking-first-step

Kuriansky, Judy. "Martin Luther King Jr. Words of Wisdom: Apply to Your Life." *Huffingtonpost.Com.*
HuffPost, 22 Mar. 2014. Web.
https://www.huffingtonpost.com/judy-kuriansky-phd/martin-luther-king-jr-wor_b_4624747.html

King, Martin Luther. "Keep Moving From This Mountain." Address at Spelman College, Atlanta,
Georgia, 10 Apr. 1960. *Kinginstitute.Stanford.Edu.* The King Institute. Web.
https://kinginstitute.stanford.edu/king-papers/documents/keep-moving-mountain-address-spelman-
college-10-april-1960

King, Martin Luther. "Remaining Awake Through a Great Revolution." Commencement Address for
Oberlin College, Oberlin, OH, June 1965. *Oberlin.Edu.* Oberlin College Archives. Web.
http://www2.oberlin.edu/external/EOG/BlackHistoryMonth/MLK/CommAddress.html

Note on Sources

"Book Tells Story of 'Hellhound' on MLK's Trail." *Jamaica-gleaner.Com.* The Gleaner, 16 May 2010.
Web.
http://jamaica-gleaner.com/gleaner/20100516/arts/arts7.html

Homans, Charles. "What the Heck is Gerald Posner Doing in Afghanistan?" *Foreignpolicy.Com.*
Foreign Policy, 6 July 2010. Web.
http://foreignpolicy.com/2010/07/06/what-the-heck-is-gerald-posner-doing-in-afghanistan/

Farmer, Ben. "Karzai Family Wealth 'Fuelling Insurgency.'" *Telegraph.Co.Uk.* The Telegraph, 7 Aug.
2009. Web.
http://www.telegraph.co.uk/news/worldnews/asia/afghanistan/5991447/Karzai-familys-wealth-fuelling-
insurgency.html

Filkins, Dexter, Mark Mazzetti and James Risen. "Brother of Afghan Leader Said to be Paid by C.I.A."
Nytimes.Com. The New York Times, 27 Oct. 2009. Web.
http://www.nytimes.com/2009/10/28/world/asia/28intel.html

Lardner, Richard. "Fraud Fighting Effort in Afghanistan Criticized." *Sandiegouniontribune.Com.* The
San Diego Union-Tribune, 14 Sept. 2011. Web.

http://www.sandiegouniontribune.com/sdut-fraud-fighting-effort-in-afghanistan-criticized-2011sep14-story.html

Risen, James. "Intrigue in Karzai Family as an Afghan Era Closes." *Nytimes.Com.* The New York Times, 3 June 2012. Web.
http://www.nytimes.com/2012/06/04/world/asia/karzai-family-moves-to-protect-its-privilege.html

"Kabul Bank Fraud Profited Elite, Leaked Audit Says."*Bbc.Com.* BBC, 28 Nov. 2012. Web.
http://www.bbc.com/news/world-south-asia-20512713

DeYoung, Karen. "Corrupt Afghan Trucking for U.S. Military Probed by Congress." *Washingtonpost.Com.* The Washington Post, 15 Sept. 2011. Web.
https://www.washingtonpost.com/world/national-security/corrupt-afghan-trucking-for-us-military-probed-by-congress/2011/09/15/gIQA9KHnVK_story.html?utm_term=.cf45ba77f3f7

Further Reading

Mayer, Jane. "Dark Money: The Hidden History of the Billionaires Behind the Rise of the Radical Right." New York: Anchor Books, 2016. Print.

Crespino, Joseph. "Strom Thurmond's America." New York: Hill and Wang, 2012. Print.

The Relentless Conservative. "The Democratic Party's Two-Facedness of Race Relations." *Huffingtonpost.com.* HuffPost, 24 Aug. 2011. Web. http://www.huffingtonpost.com/the-relentless-conservative/the-democratic-partys-two_b_933995.html

Johnson, Carrie. "The Secret Burglary That Exposed J. Edgar Hoover's FBI." *Npr.org.* National Public Radio, Inc., 7 Jan. 2014. Web. https://www.npr.org/2014/01/07/260302289/the-secret-burglary-that-exposed-j-edgar-hoovers-fbi

Hardy, Timothy S. "Intelligence Reform in the Mid-1970s." *Cia.Gov.* Central Intelligence Agency. Web. https://www.cia.gov/library/center-for-the-study-of-intelligence/kent-csi/vol20no2/html/v20i2a01p_0001.htm

Anderson, Sarah. "10 Reasons to Revive the 1968 Poor People's Campaign." *Thenation.com.* The Nation, 4 Dec. 2017. Web.
https://www.thenation.com/article/10-reasons-to-revive-the-1968-poor-peoples-campaign/

DiEugenio, James. "Destiny Betrayed: JFK, Cuba, and the Garrison Case." New York: Skyhorse Publishing, 2012. Print.

DiEugenio, James and Lisa Pease. "The Assassinations: Probe Magazine on JFK, MLK, RFK, and Malcolm X." Port Townsend: Feral House, 2012. Print.

Taylor, Alan. "Remembering Martin Luther King Jr. in Photos." *Theatlantic.Com*. The Atlantic, 19 Jan. 2015. Web. https://www.theatlantic.com/photo/2015/01/remembering-martin-luther-king-jr-in-photos/384635/

Economic Sciences Prize Committee of the Royal Swedish Academy of Sciences. "Jean Tirole: Market Power and Regulation." *Nobelprize.Org*. The Royal Swedish Academy of Sciences, 13 Oct. 2014. Web. https://www.nobelprize.org/nobel_prizes/economic-sciences/laureates/2014/advanced-economicsciences2014.pdf